Praise for *The Power of Pause*

"Nance Guilmartin reminds us all how important it is to pause and listen carefully to what our colleagues and clients are saying. A simple but powerful message in today's world."

> **—Lou Bifano,** vice president, IBM Tivoli Software

"There are times when life's going to put you in a ditch. This book helps me get out of the ditch—to rejigger my course, appreciate what I've accomplished, embrace my team, stoke my fires, and proceed on."

> **—Peter Shaplen,** *ABC World News* freelance producer

"I agree wholeheartedly with Guilmartin on the important ideas she shares in *The Power of Pause.* In the time that it takes to draw one breath, we can begin to change the world."

> **—J. Barry Griswell,** retired chairman & CEO, the Principal Financial Group, and coauthor, *The Adversity Paradox*

"Swift action can be reckless and lead us astray. Guilmartin implores us to tap into the brain's capacity to pause, reframe, and reflect before acting."

> **—Jamshed Bharucha,** provost & senior vice president, Tufts University

"This book helps us take our blinders off and gives us back the power to make a choice and not be driven by our emotions."

—**Bob Tobias,** director of public sector executive education, American University

"Reading the book gave me immediate takeaways: I had ideas for my CFO, two great ways for teams to start meetings and handle what's on our plates, and new skills to enrich my approach to performance appraisals."

—**Greg Miller,** CEO and president, CrossCom National

"*The Power of Pause* rehumanizes the workplace and gives us both thought- and action-provoking momentum to be proactive instead of reactive. Nance Guilmartin provides a framework that is just as useful in the lunchroom as it is in the boardroom or war room. Another winner!"

—**Lieutenant Colonel Edward Pfeffer,** U.S. Army, Retired

"Speaking as an IT executive, I cannot think of a better resource to provide to my staff for dealing with the decision making in a high-stress environment. Knowing that they have read this book would give me the confidence that they should be making reasoned, well-thought-out decisions, particularly in times of crisis."

—**Ramon Padilla Jr.**, assistant vice chancellor, information resources, Florida Board of Governors

"Imagine all the conflicts in a company that lead to wasted time and money. Nance Guilmartin's techniques—which you will find in this book—taught us how to break through these barriers."
   —**Joe Wyson,** executive vice president, OCEANAIR, Inc.

"The way you see and describe life today is painfully true. I admire the way each part of the book flows to the next, drawing me on to read and learn more. It is the perfect orchestration of an empowering idea that others and I can put to work, and not a moment too soon."
   —**Moshe Hammer,** founder, *From Violence to Violins*

"When it's all about the bottom line, this book is a profit accelerator and a buffer against stress. *The Power of Pause* is on time and on target."
   —**Suzie Hise,** CEO, Hise Consultants

"By using the tools Nance's book teaches, I am better able to communicate feedback to teachers simply because I now take the time to try to understand why a particular behavior occurred. I've learned not to assume that I know everything I need to know."
   —**Susan Darrow,** director of educational services, Music Together®

"The Power of Pause will help managers and coaches take the idea of helping coworkers be more effective leaders inside their organizations by providing them

with 'the' textbook for making significant positive change in their lives."

—**Joe Esparza,** cofounder, Leadership Outfitters

"It's easy to see how the book's tools can help business owners who do so much to make this country work. Why? Because—no kidding—it gives you fast, easy ways to turn a problem into an opportunity and into a greener bottom line."

—**Dan Hubbard,** owner and operator,
the UPS Store

The
POWER
of
PAUSE

How to Be More Effective
in a Demanding, 24/7 World

NANCE GUILMARTIN

JOSSEY-BASS
A Wiley Imprint
www.josseybass.com

Published by Jossey-Bass
A Wiley Imprint
989 Market Street, San Francisco, CA 94103-1741—www.josseybass.com

Power of Pause is a federally registered trademark of Nance Guilmartin.
Get Curious Not Furious is a trademark registered to Nance Guilmartin.

Jossey-Bass books and products are available through most bookstores. To contact Jossey-Bass directly call our Customer Care Department within the U.S. at 800-956-7739, outside the U.S. at 317-572-3986, or fax 317-572-4002.

Jossey-Bass also publishes its books in a variety of electronic formats. Some content that appears in print may not be available in electronic books.

Library of Congress Cataloging-in-Publication Data
Guilmartin, Nance.
    The power of pause : how to be more effective in a demanding, 24/7 world/ Nance Guilmartin.—1st ed.
        p. cm.
    Includes bibliographical references and index.
    ISBN 978-0-470-47827-1 (cloth)
        1. Public speaking. 2. Communication. I. Title.
    PN4121.G77 2010
    153.6—dc22
                                                                    2009031951

Printed in the United States of America
FIRST EDITION
HB Printing   10 9 8 7 6 5 4 3 2 1

If you wonder whether there is a better way to be effective and make a difference—in the work you do and the life you live—then this book is dedicated to you.

• • •

And these words would not have become a book without the "no excuses" encouragement of Kirk Landon, who kept saying, "Just write it down and the rest will take its course."

• • •

Now it's up to you.

CONTENTS

CONTENTS

The
POWER
of
PAUSE

AN INVITATION
TO THE
POWER OF PAUSE

Working in a nonstop world, we can go to sleep one night and wake up the next morning in a new reality. Regardless of what we do for a living or how we spend our personal time, we are no longer able to count on what we used to know or could reasonably predict. Consider these three questions. How do you:

1. Make the most of the time you have?
2. Successfully handle what's on your plate?
3. Still feel good about yourself at the end of the day?

We wonder how we'll find the time or the resilience to handle what comes at us full speed *and* to feel that we've made a difference. As one exhausted, technology-savvy business entrepreneur recently commented, "This leaves us insecure and discombobulated and brings to mind the often quoted phrase: *Stop the world I want to get off.* The trouble is that even if you did get off for a while—to collect your wits—would you know how or where to get off, or get back on?"

You don't have to get off, but you *can* pause. This book will show you ways to succeed by using that pause to plug into a different source of your own power and effectiveness. My method is called the Power of Pause®, and it's based on a paradox: to have more control over your choices and your time, you must pause—for seconds, minutes, an hour, a day, or even as briefly as a single deep breath.

It's time to see ourselves, the people we work with, our customers, *and* the challenges and opportunities around us through new lenses. If you:

- Want to be a more accomplished and effective manager or leader or simply to be able to do your best work
- Are tired of being misunderstood and wasting precious time untangling knots
- Want to initiate and promote change with less resistance, instead of tolerating an *Us* versus *Them* debate
- Want quicker ways to build trust and extraordinary relationships when you or others are pressed for time
- Want more productive results

. . . then I invite you to explore the approaches you'll find in this book. This is not about time management, nor is it about slowing the world down or unplugging from it. Instead, you'll learn a low-tech, three-step Effectiveness Equation and twelve Power of Pause practices to make every pause a productive one.

2

In sync with new research on the brain's neural plasticity, I've been teaching people to stretch beyond what they thought they knew. And I'm right there with them, which is why I'm offering you a practical framework to take action regardless of the time compression you face. It's called the Effectiveness Equation; think of it as a global positioning system to help you make better choices. It gives you a set of coordinates to *pause* (get your mental bearings), to adopt a Get Curious Not Furious™ mindset (get your emotional bearings), and to access *humility* (to go beyond what you think you know to generate a more informed response). The Effectiveness Equation takes you through three stages, which unfold throughout the book:

**Pause (Presence of Mind) + Curiosity + Humility =
Professional Effectiveness and Personal Fulfillment**

Putting this equation to work enables you to "create" additional time for yourself. It also produces an exponential effect by increasing your own impact and by raising the effectiveness of others around you, who learn by the example you set.

Why I Wrote This Book

I began to develop the empowering concepts for this book decades ago when I noticed that they helped me, and my colleagues, prevent and solve problems quickly. First, as a news writer (on a deadline), interviewing people on different sides of a story, I discovered that it was crucial to listen respectfully past their passionate positions to uncover the truths in each person's point of view. Later, as an aide to

Senator Paul Tsongas, I saw how effectively he persuaded people on opposite sides of issues to reach agreement (for example, to protect the Alaskan wilderness, innovatively restore failing cities, and protect against the threat of nuclear weapons). He was passionately committed to understanding what people's positions on these issues meant to them and to their families.

When I became editorial and communications director at Westinghouse Broadcasting, I looked for opportunities to go beyond my opinionated views. I helped introduce the practice of "doing well by doing good," originating public-private partnerships to lead national behavior change, including the *For Kids' Sake* campaign and the Designated Driver program. In the days before cause-related marketing was common practice, the *For Kids' Sake* campaign pioneered the concept of inspiring customers, sponsors, and community organizations in over one hundred U.S. cities to address local needs, as well as created a $20 million profit center for Westinghouse and its clients.

The Designated Driver program was a radical idea conceived to engage the public in a proactive approach to prevent people from drinking alcohol and driving. The idea stemmed from a series of pauses, none more important than the sadness that overwhelmed the newsroom after the death of a respected young reporter killed by a drunk driver. In the midst of what could have been a typical reaction to a tragedy—to set up a memorial fund for his widow and child, call for tougher laws, or run a series of powerful public service announcements—we stepped back; we paused to wonder what more we could do. How could we do something more powerful and longer lasting to *prevent* people from drinking and driving? This pause led us to collaborate with the Harvard School of Public Health to turn a local tragedy in Boston into a nationally recognized lifesaving campaign.

Next as a business consultant, observing increasing conflicts in the workplace, I began insisting that individuals and organizations use the Get Curious Not Furious process when things went wrong. I urged them to have the humility and wisdom to ask, *What don't I know I don't know?* I challenged them to stop looking for blame and to discover the underlying problems, hidden opportunities, and unimaginable solutions. As a result, people and teams worked better together and made progress faster.

As a communication specialist, executive coach, and educator, I have spent years in the field strengthening people's capacity to "rewire" their behaviors and adopt more constructive ways to achieve their goals. These clients have included CEOs who learned to take their companies in new directions that go beyond industry norms and their employees' comfort zones; newly promoted talent (previously superstars in their fields) who thoughtfully overcame resistance to their inexperience as managers; top hospitals that found time and cost-effective ways to support and retain their exhausted, seasoned employees; and savvy entrepreneurs who discovered better ways to attract and retain profitable customers and talent.

An Antidote to 24/7 Demands and Continuous Partial Attention

In a 24/7, fast-paced world, how do you balance
getting the job done, meeting performance levels,
while motivating others to stay in the game for
the long haul? How do you keep teams focused
on the task and desired outcome with so many
distractions? The answer is simple: Form meaningful relationships! This is impossible to do if
today's managers cannot take the time to pause,
listen, and act based on what they've learned.
— (MILLENNIAL GENERATION)
MARKETING MANAGER, FORTUNE 500 COMPANY

"Pause, listen, and act based on what they've learned."
This is good counsel. Considering the speed of what comes
at us—conflicts with colleagues that take us by surprise,
competitors breathing down our necks, a daily barrage of
information demanding a response, and time-sensitive opportunities beckoning—is it any wonder that we feel exhausted
or stressed, or don't have enough of the one thing in life that
technology and intelligence is supposed to save us? Time!

It's no surprise that when we're running low on time, we
also run out of patience, curiosity, creativity, and resilience, let
alone our sense of humor. We make mistakes, miss opportunities, and wish we could hit the rewind or fast-forward button.
We feel ambushed by "drive-by" e-mail attacks or anonymous
electronic gossip or abrupt voice mail messages. Before we know
what's happened, we have a communication breakdown.

Research reveals that we're working in a world of "continuous partial attention,"[1] prompting some of us to schedule

a weekly "secular Sabbath"[2] or "e-mail-free" Fridays. We yearn to rebalance priorities and take back time for ourselves, or to interact with people in person, rather than solely through communication devices. More of us are asking, *How can I change the way I use my time, make different choices, and still succeed?*

It's time to turn the tables on our "no time," "no choice," overwhelm-driven attitudes. Here's what the four parts of this book cover, and how their lessons will enable you to make the shift:

By the end of Part One, The Power of Pause Process
- You'll be able to suspend the urge to react on automatic and give yourself a chance to make better choices. (Please see Figure I.1.)

By the end of Part Two, Get Curious Not Furious
- You'll be able to have a productive conversation in the midst of a disagreement, or regain control when the unexpected happens, without launching personal attacks or jumping ahead with an instant answer or reactionary defense.

By the end of Part Three, What Don't I Know I Don't Know?
- You'll know how to hit your internal pause button, regroup, and discover what you didn't know you didn't know that can lead to an unimaginably successful result.

By the end of Part Four, The Art of the Pause
- You'll be putting the effectiveness and communication intelligence practices in this book to work and helping others join you, giving you more time and energy to do your best in a "Just Do It" world.

Figure 1.1. You *Have* a Choice

Something happens → You have a thought or feeling → Choose:

Pause
- OH! A moment of awareness.
- Take a moment.
- Step back.
- Take a breath.

Or

React
- Keep driving.
- Act on your feeling.
- Step on the gas.
- Sometimes you can't pause.

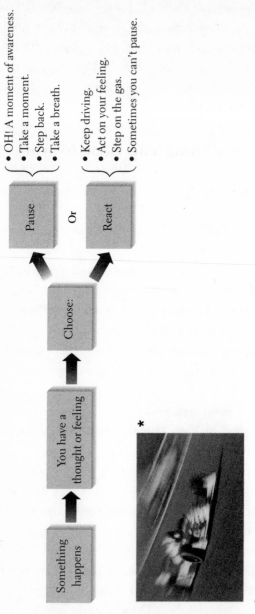

*

* Pause does not mean stop!

Suspending the urge to react instantly when the stakes are high reflects the awareness and strength of character it takes to pause—to listen, to learn, and then to lead. Making this commitment is a new way to achieve success and personal satisfaction.

Putting This Book to Work

Parts One, Two, and Three are divided into short segments on:

1. **The principles and research** that drive the Power of Pause practices
2. **True stories, case histories, and personal reflections** on how the practices work in the real world (Where indicated by an asterisk [*], names and details have been changed to protect privacy.)
3. **Putting ideas to work,** a feature that identifies practical ways to apply what you've read
4. **Tips** to help you turn these ideas into new habits you can use on your own or with others
5. **Yeah, buts,** which respond to the typical and valid questions that come with the territory of advancing new or counterintuitive ideas

Part Four takes you behind the scenes to see what happens when the Power of Pause principles are put to work by people who are succeeding against the odds—whether the obstacles are political, economic, financial, cultural, or personal. We make the journey with them from remote villages in Turkey, where there is a cancer epidemic, to the creation of an international research collaborative that unites Christians and Muslims; from a university symposium outside Boston sponsored by a low-key CEO, to peace accords in Baghdad; from launching the first improbable business-to-business Web site, to becoming one of the largest e-commerce retailers in the world; and from failure to triumph on the field, to positioning a team for the opportunity to win every game they play—right up to the last at-bat.

And if something in the book doesn't immediately apply to you, just skip ahead. As a busy executive explained, "After I know where an author is taking me, how they got there, and what's in it for me, then I can go back to read what I skipped the first time around."

Using the Power of Pause practices and the Effectiveness Equation, you can quickly become more successful, while helping others do the same no matter what comes at you at the speed of life.

PART ONE

THE POWER OF PAUSE PROCESS

HOW TO SHIFT FROM RUNNING ON AUTOMATIC

CHAPTER 1

RESTORING THE ABILITY TO CHOOSE

As an attorney representing public service workers, Bob Tobias became known for listening to both sides in a dispute and finding common ground. Today he is director of public sector executive education at American University, having retired as president of the nation's second-largest union in the federal sector. This is his story about the day he discovered the power of a single pause.

> When I first started negotiating collective bargaining agreements, I was very young and inexperienced, representing leaders who were twice my age. I was also facing the other side's chief spokesman, who was a grizzled veteran.
>
> I felt compelled—by my fear and need to impress—to interrupt and respond to any statements by the other side's chief spokesperson that disparaged my side to any degree.
>
> Although I did not smoke cigars, all of the members of my team did. So to be one of the "boys" I bought cigars, lit them, and then let them go out.

One day while I was lighting a cigar, the chief spokesperson started a diatribe, but before I could speak, he ended the diatribe with a concession.

It occurred to me that it might be a pattern; diatribe followed by concession. During the next diatribe, I overcame my fear and need to impress by lighting my cigar. A concession followed.

It was the first time that I noticed that I had a choice whether or not to respond. It was the first time that my emotion did not drive my behavior.

Bob Tobias took advantage of that pause to generate a better result. That is the "gap advantage" you gain when you exercise your power to pause.

How Do We Work When We're Living at the Edge of Time?

When we're up against a challenging person or a deadline, we're primed and instinctively programmed to react. Yet having the ability to shift gears under pressure and give ourselves the gift of a pause is one of the keys to being effective and making the best choices.

We live at the edge of time. It's the one thing most people agree on: *I don't have enough time.* Time to think. To decide. To get to the bottom of things. To get the job done right. To deal with upsets. To build quality, dependable relationships. To figure out which top priority is the *real* priority. Yet it's hard to resist the pressure to just decide, or to shake the addiction to "time-saving" devices. The ubiquitous use of instant communication technology, including cell phones, PDAs, BlackBerries, or laptops, encourages spur-of-the-moment, often ill-considered responses—like the kind you fire off just before departure when the flight attendant announces all electronic devices must be turned off, or when you are interrupted or distracted, perhaps when taking personal time with friends and family. Yet we feel pressure to respond immediately because that is what clients or colleagues—even family members—expect.

Why do we live this way? Because we don't think we have a choice! However, we *can* change the way we look at who and what's coming at us, and the way we respond by using the Power of Pause methodology. It offers a sequence of practical steps to manage our reactions and to prevent them from taking control of our decisions. First let's look at some typical situations in which our judgment is tested and we risk being overpowered by our circumstances. Remember Bob Tobias's experience and the results he achieved by choosing to pause.

What Happens When We're on Automatic?

Misunderstandings and decisions happen at the speed of our emotions. We find ourselves in this bind whether we're employers or employees, customer service agents or customers, healers or patients, or even when we're working on a virtual team with colleagues we've never met.

We're quick to say yes to someone's request because we don't think we have a choice. We just hit the Reply All or Send button on an e-mail instead of considering our options,

THE POWER OF PAUSE

picking up the phone, or walking down the hall. We jump to conclusions based on assumptions, expectations, or wished-for outcomes that are frequently far from reality. Then, working just from what we think we know, we fast-forward to make decisions, set out to prove a point, simply get rid of the problem, or take our business elsewhere. We're asked to do more with less, especially less time. We cope with these demands by shifting to automatic decision-making behavior, and we:

- Have knee-jerk reactions—emotions drive us to act before we reflect.
- Go with our gut—we follow that instant "go or no-go" feeling.
- Fall into habits—"That's how we've done it in the past."
- Persuade or delude ourselves—"I'm the boss: it's my call."
- Take it personally—*I can't believe they did that to me!*
- Assume we have no choice—"That's the best that we can do with what we have."
- Hear what we want to hear—"Maybe" means "Yes"; "No" just means "Not now."

Think about it: What did it cost you, your team, your organization, your customers, or your relationships the last time someone was misunderstood or made a snap decision that backfired? There is another way to handle what life throws at you. It starts with changing your outlook by changing what you plug into and what you tune out. I'm not talking about unplugging from technology or abandoning your to-do lists. The Power of Pause process offers a practical way to rewire your overloaded human "software" and tap back into your long-lost common sense. The following story shows what a seasoned professional decided to try when her to-do list was overwhelming.

Making Time Count

How do you make the most of the time you have—when you don't have the time you need—and end up being more successful than ever?

"Are you out of your mind?" said the nurse, as I was presenting the Power of Pause process as a quick and helpful way for busy nurses to be more effective in caring for their patients.

"Don't you know what's going on?" she cried. "There's a nursing shortage, patients need more care these days, the doctors are always busy, and now there are six different kinds of nurses on a floor, and you can't just ask anyone to help you out because they might not have the training or they might have a different degree than you and not feel it was their place or job to help! To make matters worse, when a patient gets sicker or dies, there isn't even time for nurses to deal with our own emotions."

What she was saying between the lines was clear to me and to everyone else in the room: How was she supposed to pause in the midst of all that and get her very long patient care to-do list done?

I took a deep breath, asked everyone to do the same, and then slowly let it out. Clearly this nurse was very upset at the idea of taking even a moment to catch her own breath, let alone to be with her patients or colleagues when they needed a few minutes of her time.

"It sounds like there's no way you have a minute for yourself, or anyone else," I said.

17

"Yes, you heard me loud and clear," she replied.

Then I asked her, "Would you do me a favor? I'm not sure that I have the right answer for you at this moment. I'd like to share something that I learned in preparing to speak to you today. If it answers your question, let me know. If it doesn't, we'll go from there."

The nurse nodded, sat down, and waited for me to tell my story. Here's what I said:

> When I was preparing tonight's class for your group, I was intimidated. I asked myself, *Who am I to be giving nurses any insights?* After all, I wasn't trained as a nurse, had never worked in a hospital—what was I thinking? Even though my mother was a nurse and my sister is a nurse, I knew I needed more insight than the anecdotes they'd shared with me about the challenges nurses face.
>
> So I called my friend Barbara, who had spent the past two years in and out of hospitals. She'd been diagnosed with appendiceal cancer and given six months to live. Undaunted, she was doing everything she could to live as long as possible. I told her I was teaching a professional development workshop for nurses and that they would be getting credit for it, so it had better be good. I asked her, "What is the one thing you wish I could help nurses understand better from a patient's perspective?"
>
> Barbara thought for a few minutes and then said, "Tell them that the most important thing to a patient when a nurse comes into the room—before they stick that needle in or ask us how we are doing: Could they stop and see me as a person first and a patient second? I realize they don't have enough staff to help them take care of us. And I know that they care. Here's what would be so healing that won't take but a moment. Could they soften their gaze as they look at me? As they approach my bed, could they consider whether I need a gentle touch or a positive thought that would

remind me that I am more than an item on the checklist in their understandably difficult day?"

A murmur moved across the room as the nurses were reminded that this was why they had gone into nursing. Some acknowledged that they, too, had felt like "procedures waiting to happen" while hospitalized. The nurse who'd asked the question said she appreciated my honesty and said she would think about what she could do differently.

One year later, I was back teaching another group of nurses. When I asked whether there were any questions, suddenly that same nurse raised her hand; she'd slipped in while I was speaking.

"Do you want to know what I learned to do differently?" she asked. "Here's what I do now each time before I enter the patient's room. I pause. By that I mean, all I have time for is to take a deep breath and let it out. That's all it has taken for me to remember to see the person first and the patient second. Sometimes I gently stroke their arm or shoulder before I give them medication or check to see how a wound is healing. Sometimes it feels right to give them a smile or a knowing look that acknowledges I realize that they would rather be home. That's all it takes—the time it takes me to breathe."

∞

Putting Ideas to Work

This story is about what we need to be able to do for ourselves—before we can bring our "best selves" to work or to the situation at hand. This becomes increasingly important when people feel overwhelmed by information and conflicting roles and responsibilities. We are pushed to the limit by demands that test our patience and values, and that interfere with making the right choices—whether there are too many competing interests and alternatives or too much conflicting data to process.

The nurse found a way to incorporate a pause into her routine while barely skipping a beat. In return, she was appreciated by her patients and felt more in control of a job that had seemed beyond her control. She could feel less stressed and more present and empathetic because she had found a way to take better care of her patients *and* herself.

- As a manager or a colleague, you will encounter coworkers and clients who feel overwhelmed. One way you can help them move past that feeling of paralysis is to identify a single action they can choose to take. This helps restore their sense of self-control and ability to take one step at a time.
- What kind of example could you set for others by building a strategic pause into your work routine? For example, a general manager known for always being at her desk and available to her team began routinely taking fifteen minutes for herself in the middle of the day—to regain perspective and a sense of humor, to better handle the stress she and her team faced from increased competition. As a result, her managers took the initiative to help one another solve problems during her "off-limits" pause and increased their problem-solving abilities.

CHAPTER 2

WHAT *IS* A PAUSE?

A pause can be as simple as not immediately responding to something someone says, does, or writes. It can be thirty seconds, a minute, an hour, or a day. It can be that one, deep breath. It's any space between an action and your reaction. It's the safety mechanism offering you an opportunity to make a different choice than the one you might make if you speed ahead fueled by what you *think* you know, see, or hear.

It's time to use the operating software that already exists within us—to gather our wits, review our choices, and make a more informed course correction. "A pause is *not* an opportunity to skip to another agenda item or do something else," stressed a top executive, who oversaw multibillion-dollar acquisitions involving more than eighty companies.

Advancing the interpersonal skill of "know[ing] when to set our machines aside and rely on instinct and judgment" was one of the challenges forecast when the *Harvard Business Review* asked leading thinkers about the problems business faces in the twenty-first century.[1] The experts predicted that the true test for companies wouldn't be finance, managing fixed assets, international unrest, or business hardware. The true test would be "the art of human—and humane—management."

Today you need the ability to discern what lies beneath people's words, their reactions, or their silence. If you don't build the neuropathways in your brain to pause, to momentarily disengage your automatic reactions, you can trigger a chain reaction that derails your best intentions and strategies. Relying on gut instinct to make a decision is vital, yet your intuition can get short-circuited when overpowered by demands for instant answers. Emotions can also drive illogical reactions masquerading as gut responses. That's why a pause is powerful: it restores your ability to access your intuition and to trust that what your gut is telling you works in a particular situation. It also gives you a chance to affirm your original thoughts.

By now you may be thinking, *Yes, but how can I take a time-out when everything's coming at me from all directions and my reaction time counts?* It's a fair question. The answer is, you can, and to be truly effective, you must.

Are We Asking the Right Questions?

To give you a different way of seeing the Power of Pause method as a strategic move that drives better-informed decisions, I'd like to share a story about Harold (Hal) Moore when he was a lieutenant colonel serving in Vietnam. The story is drawn from accounts of what happened when his battalion unexpectedly engaged with North Vietnamese troops. (You may recall the following events from his book *We Were Soldiers Once . . . and Young*, coauthored by war correspondent Joseph Galloway.)

Let me paint a picture of the extreme situation in which Moore exercised the discipline of a strategic pause.

It was mid-November of 1965 when he led the 450-man First Battalion, Seventh Cavalry, as the American commander on a mission into the Ia Drang Valley. The battle plan called for an air assault into a small jungle clearing called "LZ [landing zone] X-Ray." The battalion expected to encounter Viet Cong guerilla fighters; instead they were ambushed by well-trained North Vietnamese Army regulars who'd laid a trap for the Americans.

For three days, Moore's troops were engaged in a bloody jungle assault against an estimated two thousand North Vietnamese Army fighters. Sharpshooters first targeted the cavalry's officers, their radiomen, and then anyone who moved. For two days, one platoon of twenty-nine Americans was cut off, surrounded by two hundred of the enemy; another unit lost every one of its officers. Moore had to constantly adapt his strategy and tactics, calling for reinforcements and massive air and artillery fire support as his troops fought back around the clock, sometimes outmanned seven to one.

In spite of overwhelming odds, none of Moore's men was taken prisoner; he reported that 79 were killed and 121 were wounded. The enemy body count was 634, with an estimated 1,215 additional North Vietnamese killed or wounded. In spite of their losses, both sides claimed victory in the fierce battle, which tested their ability to fight a new kind of war.

In a lengthy After Action Report, Moore debriefed his colleagues about the costly lessons learned so that they could adapt their tactics to fighting this unfamiliar enemy. (This, too, is a strategic pause: debriefing what worked or didn't work before moving on to what's next.) He concluded by mentioning his discipline of focused reflection in the middle of chaos: "The commander on the battlefield must

23

continually anticipate what the future may bring or could bring and take steps to influence the future before it comes about. . . . Also, periodically throughout a battle, the commander must mentally detach himself from the action and objectively think—what is not being done which should be done to influence the situation, and what is being done which should not be going on."[2]

What impressed me most about the lieutenant colonel's actions was that he had the *presence of mind* to pause. Here was someone in the heat of battle, who instead of charging forward, did something counterintuitive: he stepped back. He emotionally disengaged—for seconds—in order to reflect, and had the humility to ask himself, *What is happening? What is not happening? What can I do to change the outcome in my favor?*[3]

When faced in business with overwhelming odds, surprise, urgency, and the need to constantly adapt your strategy, you can momentarily detach yourself mentally from the action—to ask better questions, listen with an open mind, and objectively consider your options. One of the Power of Pause practices is to ask yourself, *What don't I know I don't know?* Moore's account shows you how seamlessly the Effectiveness Equation,

Pause (Presence of Mind) + Curiosity + Humility = Professional Effectiveness and Personal Fulfillment

can work to identify the best options in the time you have, even in the most challenging situations.

The following case study demonstrates how much more effective you can be in business when you step back to ask the right questions, even when you're taken by surprise.

24

The Power of Pause in Action—with a Team and a Top Client

How do you discover that the real problem isn't what you thought *or* what your client first told you, and then generate a solution in twenty-four hours?

What are your options when you think your team and a top client are on the same page, then suddenly they've changed their mind about an agreement? That's what happened at a Fortune 500 company one afternoon, just before the presses were ready to roll. Here's how the story unfolded as told by a marketing manager (we'll call her JoAnne*); her company, K&S; and its client Acme, Inc.

❧

JoAnne Sets the Stage

In February 2008, Acme, Inc., gave JoAnne's company permission to do a case study profiling its supply chain operation and the solutions that K&S provided. She explained, "We use these 'Spotlight' studies in marketing and communication initiatives to benefit our customer and us. When the customer approves the completed profile, we also have them sign a legally binding consent form allowing us to use any of the profile material in future marketing and communications initiatives. Acme had repeatedly told us they were happy with the results we'd delivered and had already joined us in several press events."

What Happened?

Immediately after JoAnne finalized the Acme Spotlight and got its signed consent form, K&S persuaded *Business Today*, a trade press publication, to do a story based on a reformatting of the profile.

After submitting the piece to the magazine, which the consent form authorized JoAnne to do, she sent this e-mail to the client:

> Hi, Rob!
>
> I have great news—we have our first press opportunity to leverage the Acme Spotlight case study that we just finalized.
>
> I wanted to let you know that the attached (see PDF) will run in the May edition of *Business Today* magazine.
>
> I hope you are well, we'll talk soon, I'm sure, JoAnne

The client sent an e-mail the next day saying this:

> JoAnne,
>
> Although I understand the intent of what K&S is doing, I am little disappointed that this was not run by Skip and me first. Skip and I have been very willing and able to support the press opportunities, but it is getting overwhelming, and may bring unwanted attention our way.
>
> Additionally, and not necessarily the main point, we made some concessions in this article, specifically when using the term "dysfunction," that we would not necessarily want out to the masses.
>
> My intent is not to shoot the messenger here, but is there a way to stop this in this current issue? If not, please make sure everything is reviewed with us prior to the release.
>
> Thanks, Rob

What's at Stake? Reputation!

The client's request that she stop the story from being published took JoAnne by surprise. "First, the story had already been submitted, and my gut told me it would be very difficult to revoke it. Second, even if I was able to revoke the story, I did not have another one to run in its place. Third, the story coverage was part of a larger campaign that K&S was running, and revoking it would jeopardize this campaign."

WHAT *IS* A PAUSE?

The Power of Pause

JoAnne knew the cost of instantly replying to someone who is upset. "I have learned the hard way that responding immediately to e-mails that pose conflict can be extremely detrimental. E-mails sent in the heat of the moment can provoke emotionally charged responses that are often based on faulty assumptions or conclusions. So, upon receiving the client's response . . . I paused."

What's Happening? What's Not Happening?

She decided to quickly start investigating. "I called the client's account manager, Matt, and my boss, to understand any external factors that I didn't know about. I kept asking, 'Did something happen to sour our relationship with the customer?' The answer from all fronts was no! Acme was still on good terms with us. Why Rob had responded so curtly was still a mystery."

After this pause, she was ready to reread the client's e-mail. She began to ask herself some pointed questions.

I noticed that in the first paragraph Rob used the term "unwanted attention." Did this mean unwanted attention to Acme as a company? To the company's supply chain? Or to Rob and Skip as individuals? In the second paragraph, the client clearly had an unresolved issue with the final version of the Spotlight piece, despite having signed the consent form. What had we done wrong in the revision and approval process? Finally, in the third paragraph, he asked me to take action to revoke the article. Why revoke it completely? Why not simply revise the content with something the client felt comfortable with? In short, there were lots of questions that needed answers before I felt comfortable responding to the client's requests. I also needed to figure out a way to convince them to run the article, since the story had already gone to the press.

Surfacing the "Hidden" Problem

Her team decided to take a back-door approach to the situation. "Due to his personal relationship with the customer, Matt decided to wait twenty-four hours and then call Rob to have a heart-to-heart conversation. Matt began the conversation by saying how surprised he was that Rob objected to a press opportunity that he would have eagerly embraced a few months ago. Rob immediately apologized, saying, "Matt, you're right. I had a knee-jerk reaction to JoAnne's e-mail, and it was not fair to her. K&S has gone a long way to help Acme, and we really appreciate that. But I have to be honest: the positive attention that my boss and I get as a result of the media coverage can be very uncomfortable. Some of our coworkers, who work equally hard, are starting to resent us a bit. We're also beginning to be held to a higher level of performance by our superiors; now everyone will expect those types of results from us."

The Outcome

The customer was upset because too many good things were happening! When all was said and done, the client let K&S run the story. However, now JoAnne's company can better balance the individual needs the two managers have (to share credit) and the company's interest in publicity.

It's unlikely that the K&S team would have imagined that the client's objections stemmed from receiving too much positive attention. Pausing gave the team a chance to put their defensive reactions on hold and find nuggets of buried information that shifted their relationship to be more powerfully in sync. Clearly there are reasons why clients don't pick up the phone to alert us to potentially embarrassing concerns. That's where your opportunity lies—to uncover problems before they escalate.

Putting Ideas to Work

- What type of standard "early warning" agreement could you set up with your clients to make you and them more comfortable about quickly surfacing a potential problem? For example, one of my clients has a "Bill of Rights" that it reviews with new clients. It spells out a process for handling complaints and concerns—as they emerge—before someone reaches a breaking point.

- When you need to explore a possible problem with a client, what can you do to make sure that your opening remarks don't set off a defensive reaction? (Consider Matt's selection of the phrase, "I was surprised when . . ." and how easy that made it for his customer to tell him the real story.)

POWER OF PAUSE PRACTICE #1:
Drive Your Choices Instead of Being Driven

As we saw with Lieutenant Colonel Moore, it takes discipline to step back to scan your options, especially when you least feel you have minutes to spare. One way to develop that control is to use a mental shortcut—similar to the process we use to drive a car—to jump-start a pause.

Imagine you are behind the wheel of a high-performance car. Unlike an automatic transmission—where all you do is turn on the ignition, step on the gas, and go—a stick shift requires you to:

1. Briefly ease your foot *off* the gas
2. Momentarily disengage the gears by pushing down on the clutch

3. Move the gear-shift lever through neutral
4. Engage the correct gear
5. Smoothly reengage the clutch by lifting your foot
6. Accelerate

The pause takes only a split second, and when you do it expertly, you are able to apply maximum engine power to the wheels. Effective communication and decision making are a lot like that. Briefly disengaging the clutch is a pause, which allows for quickly passing through neutral, as you can see in Figure 2.1. How would this process work if we were talking about your communication or decision making? The Power of Pause process gives you a chance to consider better options that you cannot see (or hear) if you are stepping on the gas, driven by stress, assumptions, or high-powered urges to react. When you drive your conversations and decision making using these six steps—to manage emotional energy and to take back the self-control that's needed to exercise better choices—you are using the Power of Pause process.

Around the world, the 24/7 workday finds many of us juggling demands for high-speed decisions in the face of fewer resources and high expectations. Powered by technology that prompts reactions at the speed of a click, we're left feeling that we can't stop to catch our breath. Yet it's worth taking a moment to consider that the effects of stress on efficiency have been studied in the workplace for over a hundred years. Research done by Dr. Herbert Benson sheds light on the strategic value of inserting a pause when faced with the need to react. He leverages stress by counteracting it with a simple sudden distraction that he calls the relaxation response: "by completely letting go of a problem at that

Figure 2.1. Choices Have Consequences

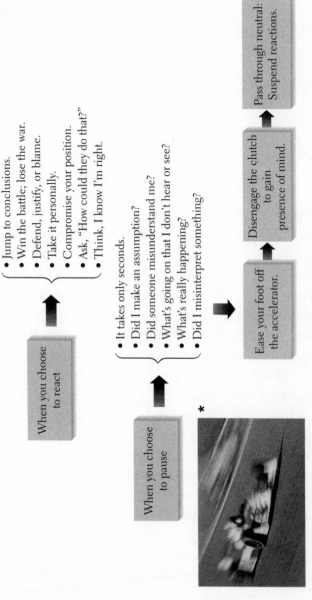

When you choose to react
- Jump to conclusions.
- Win the battle; lose the war.
- Defend, justify, or blame.
- Take it personally.
- Compromise your position.
- Ask, "How could they do that?"
- Think, I know I'm right.

When you choose to pause
- It takes only seconds.
- Did I make an assumption?
- Did someone misunderstand me?
- What's going on that I don't hear or see?
- What's really happening?
- Did I misinterpret something?

Ease your foot off the accelerator.

Disengage the clutch to gain presence of mind.

Pass through neutral: Suspend reactions.

*The race car is still moving; the goal is the same; focus on the finish line!

THE POWER OF PAUSE

[stress] point by applying certain triggers, the brain actually rearranges itself so that the hemispheres communicate better. Then the brain is better able to solve the problem. . . . As the brain quiets down, another phenomenon that we call 'calm commotion' or a focused increase in activity takes place in the areas of the brain associated with attention, space-time concepts and decision making."[4]

Stripping the Gears

Returning to the metaphor of the race car, consider the consequences if we don't properly use the clutch to briefly disengage and choose the right gear: the engine isn't effectively transferring its power to the car's wheels. Even if you've never driven a stick shift, you've heard that sound before—the sound of gears grinding because they're not in sync.

The same happens in real life when we're driving ourselves or others to get something done fast. Suddenly we find we've "stripped the gears." Our communication isn't in sync; we're not connecting. The result? We suffer what I call "drive-by" conversations. You know the feeling. It's when you assume that what you heard is what someone meant. You speak, he speaks. You think you understand; he thinks he was clear. You think: *mission accomplished*. And these drive-by conversations happen regardless of whether we're having them face-to-face, over the phone, or in the electronic digital universe.

It's also worth noting that race-car drivers, when they disengage the clutch, can actually pause the process long enough, a split second, to hear the engine and efficiently transfer the engine's power smoothly to the car's wheels. They use that pause to their advantage. A business executive who is an expert in both mentoring high-performance people and driving high-performance cars explained, "The power of a pause, whether you are driving yourself or driving a car, is that a pause is an energy conversion mechanism. It only works if it's done in sync. A car will stall if you try to start out from zero in fourth gear; so will important communication."

Unlike a race car driver, who is consciously shifting in and out of four or five gears to ensure that precisely the right gear is engaged, much of the time we're driving our lives on automatic—missing the opportunity to apply our power more effectively.

If we're not in sync, sooner or later we *will* grind our gears. When we're out of sync with others, the wear and tear on us is cumulative, too. It can show up as lost profits or fewer customers, as stress or serious illness, or in missed opportunities and frayed relationships. Even the most adept racecar driver does not simply put the pedal to the metal and never let up; nor should we.

CHAPTER 3

THE PARADOX OF PAUSE

YOU GAIN IMPACT BY TAKING A (BRIEF) TIME-OUT

I t's a paradox: to move forward, you gain time and options if you momentarily ease *off* the accelerator, suspend your initial reactions, and consider your immediate assumptions. Here's how one senior manager in state government uses the paradox of a pause to help a fast-moving team be even more productive:

> In adrenaline-pumping moments, pausing is the furthest thing from anyone's mind. But it is exactly what they need to do. People can get hung up on timing, but a pause doesn't have to take forever. If you are good at it (and it is a skill that has to be developed—kind of like triage), you can get it done very rapidly, and people leave the moment feeling that at least you have things under control.
> I do this all the time in meetings and usually begin with, "Forgive me for taking a second or two here, but

I want to try and rephrase-recap what I think I understand, what we as a group just said, and what we have
decided to do." This usually leads to a five-minute
time-out where heads can cool, and people listen and
make corrections if needed. Then the group either
moves on with a consensus of opinion or realizes that
everyone was *not* on the same page and the issue
needs to be readdressed. I tend to do this when I feel
like a meeting is out of control or something just
happened that doesn't sit right with me intellectually
and I need more explanation to wrap my head around
the issue.

Another example of the paradoxical power of a pause
is this: when you exercise the presence of mind to pause,
your ability to make better choices is sharpened, and that
can lead to significantly better results for you and for your
clients. Exercising the self-control to pause and make different choices also increases your communication intelligence,
a concept we'll explore in the next section. Let's first look at
the competitive field of law for an example of how a pause
restores your power when responding to someone who's
pressuring you to act fast.

Ellen* is a prominent securities attorney whose colleague
asked for her expert eye and quick review of a client's proposal
for a public offering. Ellen had a "funny feeling"—sensing
there might be something incorrect or incomplete—and
insisted on having more data. She resisted her colleague's
argument that her expertise should be sufficient to provide a
fast review. At first he dismissed her need for more information,
giving her the impression that he thought she ought to be "an
instant genius."

However, she had the presence of mind to pause again—to reassure him that even though his proposal *was* logical, the reason she couldn't just say yes was that no one had ever asked her to present regulators with a deal structured like this one. She could not predict how they would react to his plan.

She explained to me, "Your Power of Pause process helped me resist the pressure to satisfy my colleague's demands that I provide an instant answer that *appeared* to solve his situation. Instead, with the additional information, I had a chance to identify a problem no one else had known existed and, therefore, gave better legal advice to our client. **However, the 'instant solution' would have been a false solution.**"

Ellen said yes to a better outcome and no to the intimidation that she ignore the need for crucial information. By momentarily putting in the clutch, she changed the dynamic in the relationship. She was able to disengage from her colleague's anxiety, giving him an unexpected chance to rethink his priorities and collect the additional data.

People have asked me, "How is a pause powerful, especially when your reputation or your job is at risk if you don't respond fast enough?" Ellen's story shows how a choice to take a measured moment restored her power to say no when she felt pressured to say yes. As author William Ury explains in *The Power of a Positive No*, when you take the time to communicate what you are saying yes to, it enables you to provide someone with a more effective no.[1] In Ellen's case it prevented a mistake that would have taken a toll in time, money, and the reputations of the two attorneys, their company, and also their client.

What's Your CQ?

A high IQ is not enough to succeed today; we also have to have high *communication intelligence,* or what I call CQ. What I mean by communication intelligence is demonstrating the agility to:

- Correctly interpret incoming information and exercise the self-control to listen
- Confirm that you understood what the other person meant
- Accurately convey meaningful thoughts, ideas, and messages
- Confirm that what you meant was understood the way you intended

It's this simple. Exercising CQ means that you: speak clearly, listen closely, rephrase with an open mind, and take responsibility—up front—for being understood. Don't assume anything just because you think you were clear.

CQ begins with cultivating a focused state of mind— one that some refer to as mindfulness—as an antidote to the instant urge to react.

When we react on automatic, we're not operating with all our ability. When we're caught off guard or pressured, it's hard to say what we really mean. And it gets worse. We hardly listen to what other people say to us. No wonder we often don't feel heard, much less understood. It's generally accepted that about 70 to 80 percent of verbal communication gets "ignored, misunderstood or quickly forgotten."[2] Judging from that statistic and your own experience, you might think to yourself, *Is what you said what I heard and what I heard what you meant, and did you understand what I meant to say to you?*

Who's on First?

One of my favorite examples of how easily communication can be hijacked—misconstrued without immediately understanding that something has gone wrong—is Abbott and Costello's famous 1930s baseball comedy routine, "Who's on First?" It's a classic example (worth listening to)[3] that has been translated into many languages and was even performed for President Franklin Roosevelt. It reminds us of what can easily go wrong when one person thinks he is perfectly clear about what he is saying and the other person—with good reason—has a totally different understanding of what is being said. Here are a few lines from one of the many versions of their performance. The rapid-fire dialogue takes place when Costello asks his friend Abbott to tell him the names of the players and which position they play on the [fictional] baseball team Abbott is coaching. The conversation quickly becomes infuriating to Costello because he has no context for understanding that, as odd as it sounds, the first baseman's name is actually *Who*:

> Costello: Well then who's on first?
> Abbott: Yes.
> Costello: I mean the fellow's name.
> Abbott: Who.
> Costello: The guy on first.
> Abbott: Who.
> Costello: The first baseman.

Abbott: Who.
Costello: The guy playing.
Abbott: Who is on first!
Costello: I'm asking YOU who's on first.

● ● ●

One key component of CQ is foresight—taking responsibility ahead of time to prevent yourself from being misunderstood. This means that you are alert to the potential for ambiguity. Armed with that awareness, you give people a clue as to what you mean—just as I did at the start of this section when, aware that the term "communication intelligence" can also refer to information gathering for military purposes, I clarified what I meant. In Abbott's case, given the oddity of the player's name, he could have anticipated the likelihood of confusion and averted this communication hijacking by explaining, "Who is on first base. What I mean is that the player on first base has an unusual name; his name is actually Who."

Boosting communication intelligence requires being committed to something greater than thinking that you are perfectly clear or insisting that you are right. It means that you pay attention to the "communion" in communication: the *two-way exchange* of words, thoughts, energy, and the unspoken. You choose to step back to get curious about where the other person is coming from, *especially* if she is confused, difficult, competing for advantage, or worse.

Communication isn't complete just because you said it or sent it; it's only complete when you take responsibility for making sure that the message was received and understood in the way that you intended. This, too, is a sign of CQ in action.

Your Mindset Drives Results and Raises CQ

Another aspect of communication intelligence is your ability to adjust your frame of reference, otherwise known as your *mindset*. Your willingness to change the way you interpret information, especially when you think you are correct or could justifiably rely on experience, is another way to raise your CQ. As we saw in the stories about Lieutenant Colonel Moore and the marketing manager (in Chapter Two) and the securities attorney, it takes discipline, curiosity, a little courage—and some pride swallowing—to check your assumptions before you formulate an effective response for others to follow, especially when there's a lot at stake.

The practice of being curious is more than simply being inquisitive or exhaustively seeking detailed data. In Part Two we'll take a look at the results you can achieve when you combine the discipline of a brief pause with curiosity. As you'll see throughout the book, that's the Power of Pause process in action, part of the Effectiveness Equation, which presents you with a new framework for achieving your goals. The equation focuses effort on generating more productive results, rather than on just getting results faster or being better than someone else:

Pause (Presence of Mind) + Curiosity + Humility = Professional Effectiveness and Personal Fulfillment

You may be wondering exactly what I mean by humility. It goes beyond a lack of self-importance. The extra dimension of humility that is so powerful in today's "on-demand" times is this: in situations where you think you know enough, pausing to wonder what you *don't* know is a vital, even game-changing leadership skill. This skill is important when you need to uncover the root causes of a complex problem or want to generate new solutions.

Having the discipline to pause gives you an advantage. It's your choice: Do you let people and circumstances drive you, or do you retain self-control? It all starts with your outlook. As the saying goes, *Where you start out determines where you end up.* I first learned the effect of adopting this mindset when I was working with John Scherer, a colleague and the author of *The Five Questions That Change Everything.* He never lets you forget that the attitude you start out with has everything to do with how things turn out in the end. It's your intention that drives your attention. And the quality of our attention, in a distraction-filled life, determines what we hear, what we see, and what we *think* someone meant. The next story shows how to put these ideas into practice when you feel blindsided.

Who Does He Think He Is? (Part 1)
What do you do when you think someone one-upped you?

There are no doubt times when you feel that someone is out to get you. Emotions take over, and it's hard to get past your outrage at what you think the person is doing to you. How are you supposed to pause when you want to attack or when you feel entitled to get even or at least to prove that the other person is wrong? This story is about what happened when a senior executive turned to his executive coach to keep from driving his career off the cliff. You never know when you might need a fast way either to step back from the brink of making the wrong decision or to help someone else resist the urge to jump to conclusions.

∞

Your telephone rings. The person on the other end of the line is a furious client under the gun to respond. Now *you're* on the spot because he's counting on you to keep him from going off half-cocked and doing something he'll regret. What do you do?

That's the situation that an experienced executive coach faced one evening when her client called. She had been hired to help a fairly new top executive smooth his transition to overseeing the rapid expansion of a multimillion-dollar division at his organization. Some of the longtime employees were complaining about the way George* had been making changes. He hit the wall that night when he felt caught in a power play with John, a peer whose tenure at the organization was the source of enormous political clout.

The incident took place at a budget meeting where, without warning, George heard John, who had been the former division chief, announce that millions of dollars would be taken out of George's budget and spent to buy new equipment—without putting the contract out for a competitive bid. Just like that, in front of other members of the department, George's authority had been challenged.

"Who did this guy think he was?" George yelled at his coach. "He can't do this to me! I'm in charge of this project, and they hired me to shape things up, not run them the way John used to do."

In this new job, George knew he was expected to be in control of the project *and* himself. Today his anger had silenced him. He felt powerless. To make matters worse, he'd just gotten a Friday-night e-mail from John announcing that *he* was taking control of the multimillion-dollar deal that George was supposed to be overseeing. Now he felt that he had no choice but to do something before it was too late.

What could he do?

- He could fire back an e-mail to John, telling him that he was out of line and that the decision wasn't his to make.
- He could call John and ask him, "What were you thinking?"
- He could call his boss and ask him, "What the hell is going on?"
- He could circulate his own plan, which was to allocate the funds based on instituting a competitive bidding requirement, something that would make everyone realize just how behind the times the company had been when John was in charge.

He thought about those options as well as a few more that are unprintable here. Instead, he put those ideas on hold, resisted the urge to react, and called his coach to get advice.

"This would never have happened to me at the other organizations I've run," he told his coach. "What kind of place are they operating here? I've already decided to switch to a competitive bidding process because that's what we need now that we're a larger organization. That's my call. I'm the one responsible for making this new division work. That's why they recruited me and put me in charge."

At this point he was yelling and cursing. His coach knew that George needed to catch his breath, and so did she. It would be so easy to get caught up—emotionally entrained—in his need to take action. So she asked him to tell her a little more: "OK, tell me, what did you do at the meeting when this happened?"

"I was so angry I couldn't even speak," he told her. He'd been shocked into silence.

"What are we dealing with right now?" she asked, helping him focus on one problem at a time.

He explained, "The reason I've called you this late is that I've just gotten an e-mail from John. He sent it to everyone at the meeting to confirm that he's going through with awarding the contract to the vendor he used when he was in charge. I want to confront him and tell him, 'Keep your f-ing hands out of my budget. I'm in charge now, not you.' But I know I can't do that, so what can I do?"

Having taken several Power of Pause workshops, the coach knew that to provide effective counsel she had to avoid reacting to her client's anxiety. "I had to pause myself," she explained to me later, "because it's easy to get caught up in someone else's panic or crisis. I knew that I had to help him to see the bigger picture instead of assuming this was a personal attack."

Putting Ideas to Work

- How easy would it be for you to ask someone for advice when you are furious, embarrassed, and sure you are right and have done nothing wrong? What is one thing you could do that would help slow your impulse to jump to conclusions?
- What might you do differently the next time someone who is furious corners you for advice when she feels certain she has been wronged and is determined to even the score?

This story continues in Chapter Four. In this opening segment, you've seen how to slow down the impulse to react out of anger. When the story continues in Part Two, you'll hear how in fifteen more minutes that same night, his coach taught George to see beyond his anger. He took his relationship with a colleague from a breakdown to an unimaginable breakthrough. (If you want to finish the story right now, just turn to page 60.)

TIPS AND *YEAH, BUTS*

The stories throughout the book show how pausing to check your initial reaction can save time and save face in the end. The question is, *How do you spot the cues that signal it's time to pause, especially when you don't feel that you have the time or the need?* I've developed this list of cues as tips to alert you to when to pause and to activate your CQ.

Cues That a Pause Is in Your Interest

If you are thinking, feeling, or saying any of the following, it's time to pause.

1. *I have no choice.*

Step toward a pause by asking yourself, *What would I do if I did have a choice?* You could also consider the point of view that we always have a choice even if we feel that we don't. Of course there are consequences to the choices we make—some better than others. Even doing nothing is a choice.

Reclaiming the power to choose how we respond to what is going on around us is one of the key principles underlying the Power of Pause practices.

The idea that we always have a choice—even when we feel that we don't—is a powerful one. Holocaust survivor Dr. Victor Frankl made an unforgettable case for this point of view in his book *Man's Search for Meaning*. He was asked whether a concentration camp survivor can mentally escape his surroundings. He answers, "We who lived in concentration camps can remember the men who walked through the huts comforting others, giving away their last piece of bread. They may have been few in number, but they offer sufficient proof that everything can be taken from a man but one thing: the last of human freedoms—to choose one's attitude, in any given set of circumstances, to choose one's way."[1] This passage inspires me to remember that even in the worst of circumstances, when we don't think we have a choice, we do.

2. *This doesn't make sense. How could he-she-they do that (to me)?*

This reaction signals that something doesn't make sense to you given what you expected or had experienced in the past. Take a pause to ask yourself, *What am I or they missing?*

3. *I have to act now or else "they" will beat me to it.*

At the very least, call a short break, walk around the block, or if you can, sleep on it. Dr. Thomas Crook, former research director for the National Institute of Mental Health, recently reported new research about how the brain integrates problems and options by sorting through old and new information during deep slow wave sleep.[2]

4. *I can't believe this is happening again!*

Ask yourself, *What's the pattern that I haven't noticed before or that I've ignored, hoping it would go away?*

5. *We're not on the same page.*

Ask yourself, *Am I sure that they've understood my intentions, and vice versa?*

47

6. *This isn't what I expected.*

Step back and ask yourself, *What assumptions am I making? What assumptions did they make?* Once you've got those ideas, think about whether it makes sense to start over. Much as races have false starts when someone jumps the gun, so do we.

7. *I know the answer, and I'm not interested in what someone else thinks.*

When you're sure you're right about something, aren't open to input, and are about to dive into action, instead consider, *What might another perspective offer me?* The key here is to check to make sure that you are at least open to another point of view rather than being dogmatic or self-righteous.

Yeah, Buts . . . on Pausing

After years of advising and teaching professionals, I've come to value those inevitable moments in the process of introducing new ideas when participants say, "Yeah, but . . ." In the context of introducing an idea, as an educator I see *Yeah, buts* as an opportunity to address valid concerns and misconceptions. (However, I urge you to resist saying "Yes, but . . ." in the everyday course of communication when you may automatically utter those words to take issue with what someone said. Anything you say after the word "but" discounts what another person said, reducing the chance for a productive communication. At those times, I suggest that you pause to consider a better course of action, whether that is checking your assumptions or rephrasing, which we'll cover in Part Two.)

Here are several common misconceptions about the counterintuitive concept that pausing is a way to *recapture* time and power, along with workplace-tested counterpoints to consider.

•••

Yeah, but #1: It takes too much time.
Reality: A pause can be a few minutes or even seconds. You decide.

- Your pause can be ten minutes, half–an–hour, or fifteen seconds of focused reflection. In that time, you can give yourself or someone else permission to play the devil's advocate, questioning assumptions with no holds barred. Or bring in an expert who doesn't have a primary stake in your situation, to ask questions you might not consider.

- A pause can *save* you time. Consider the time it takes to clear up a misunderstanding. Communication snafus happen more often than we realize because it's so easy to hear what we want to hear or to solve what we *think* the problem is, and move on. The chain reaction of one wrong assumption takes *a lot more time* to deal with down the road than would clarifying it from the start.

- A pause can make you more successful. By momentarily slowing down, you consider your options, rethink your assumptions, and give yourself a chance to generate a better result without stripping the gears.

***Yeah, but* #2: You can look indecisive when you pause.**
Reality: Pausing can be a sign of strength.

- I'm not suggesting that you unnecessarily delay decisions or procrastinate—for example, because you don't have all the data you want or because you hope you can avoid making a difficult choice by waiting for the problem to resolve itself. Leadership today involves making decisions when all the time you have is all the time you are going to get. Like Lieutenant Colonel Moore, you must make a choice that yields you the best result.
- Giving yourself even a one-minute pause to confirm your understanding about what you are dealing with, or to clarify the best available choice given the options, can lead to a breakthrough that opens new doors. (We'll be talking more about this skill in Part Two.)
- You can give others your rationale for temporarily suspending a decision. Doing so lets them know why you are doing this and that you aren't just stuck in "analysis paralysis."

***Yeah, but* #3: How can you stay competitive if you pause?**
Reality: A pause can give you the competitive edge.

"How do we pause when the competition is beating down the door?" asked a chief operating officer. His question goes straight to the bottom-line paradox of decision making in a 24/7 economy. Competitors can launch an initiative or an attack at the speed of a computer keystroke, yet there are times when a pause can give you an advantage.

- When competitors are beating down the door or worse, take a pause to ask the questions *What aren't we thinking of in our rush to act? If we had more time, what would we do?* Don't focus on the time you don't have. Focus on what you think would be possible if you had more time. Once you have that idea in hand, see whether it's possible to start moving in that direction, to begin to leverage existing resources or mobilize additional ones.

- Another way to resist the pressure to react is to consider this perspective on the relationship between stress and time, suggested by Stefan Klein, physicist and time perception expert. Klein refutes the common interpretation of Benjamin Franklin's oft-quoted phrase "time is money." He explains that Franklin didn't mean for us to adopt the attitude that we must make every second count; he only meant that we shouldn't "sit idle." Klein points out that "Believing time is money to lose, we perceive our shortage of time as stressful. . . . We are not stressed because we have no time. We have no time because we are stressed."[3]

What's Next? How to Take Back Control and Get New Options

Throughout Part One, you've learned there is power in pausing—the first part of the Effectiveness Equation. In Part Two, you'll learn about the next part of the equation, the role that curiosity plays in your effectiveness. When you combine the elements in the equation, you will be more effective because you'll spend less time clearing up communication miscues. You'll be more responsive, in sync with others, and focused on solving the real problem rather than wasting time reacting to surface issues.

51

I'm asking you to rethink the ways you approach your work and life so that as you move forward—with great purpose—you spend less time reacting on automatic. Here's a visual cue that may reinforce your choices.

Keep Yourself from Driving Off the Cliff

Think of the classic Roadrunner cartoon and imagine the Power of Pause as the safety mechanism to save you from one more Wile E. Coyote moment of life. Wile E. is that poor coyote who is always running off a cliff while in pursuit of the elusive Roadrunner.

Wile E. Coyote moments can happen any time we fail to pause, only to discover ourselves just beyond the edge of the cliff, staring down thousands of feet into the abyss, knowing that the impending free fall will certainly be painful!

Wile E. never paused, and look what happened to him—episode after episode. He was reborn to pursue his quest thanks only to the animator's pen.

How's your ink supply? Running on empty? Needing a refill? Read on.

PART TWO

GET CURIOUS NOT FURIOUS

TAKE BACK CONTROL TO GET NEW OPTIONS

CHAPTER 4

WHAT HAPPENS WHEN WE'RE WIRED TO SNAP?

This is today's challenge: in our rush, we don't realize that we've missed something important—a fact, an intention, a tone, a subtle expression, an unperceived issue, history, or a new reality. Later we wish we'd taken even a moment to ensure that what we thought we understood was what someone really meant. What's lost is priceless: the power of curiosity in action.

From the moment the day begins, we are juggling work and our personal lives. Before we know it, we're making snap decisions or we're snapping at each other. When we don't feel that we have the time *or* the need to get curious we can (1) get angry or defensive or (2) make hasty decisions.

Working and living at this pace, we can unwittingly trigger a costly chain reaction that sends customers running to the competition or charging to the Internet to complain. We can unleash reactions that fan the flames of employee or investor rumors and cost us, or someone else, a job. Or, when we feel we're right, defending our assumptions can suddenly

55

threaten a valued relationship. If, however, we can shift into neutral and become *genuinely* curious, we can prevent a costly mistake.

It's so easy to forget: *most upsets are the result of unexpressed or misunderstood expectations.*[1] Numerous research studies reveal that expectations shape what we see, hear, sense, and value. In a study published in the *Journal of Marketing Research*, authors Baba Shiv, Ziv Carmon, and Dan Ariely pointed out that our reality is shaped by our expectations. For example, when research subjects were told that an item they were given to use was expensive, they thought that it worked better than those participants who were told that the products they were using were inexpensive. However, the products were exactly the same.[2] We're also surprised when something *isn't* what we anticipated or were led to believe. A pause can "reset" us to neutral. Then we'll be more effective when the unexpected happens.

At this point, you might be thinking to yourself, *OK, so now that it's time to shift, the clutch is disengaged, my foot is off the accelerator—what am I supposed to do with this pause? In the real world, I do need to get going—to get others and myself in gear, jump-start a project, or give someone an answer. I'm expected to get it together and move on, and it had better be right the first time.*

You're absolutely right. The urge to act makes it hard to put our brain and emotions on hold or to insert a pause rather than automatically react. In a *Boston Globe* article, Jonah Lehrer, author of *How We Decide*, explains that experts are seeing the act of decision making with fresh eyes, suggesting that "the best predictor of good judgment isn't intuition or experience or intelligence. Rather it's the willingness to engage in introspection, to cultivate what Philip Tetlock, a psychologist at the University of California, Berkeley, calls 'the art of self-overhearing.'"[3]

How *can* you engage in introspection, especially when you're under pressure to react? The next segments of this chapter show you how to suspend your reactions just long enough to get curious and explore what lies beneath what you think you heard or sensed. Before we consider that reflective mindset, though, let's look at what sparks reactions and drives snap decisions.

Curiosity Doesn't Come Naturally . . . After We Grow Up

Most of us would agree that small children are curious by nature. They're not driven by what they already know, and they aren't worried about being wrong or right. It doesn't take long, though, before they learn which behaviors are rewarded and which behaviors cause pain.

In his book *Emotional Intelligence*, psychologist Daniel Goleman gave us the term "emotional hijacking." That's when our biology overpowers reason and triggers an emotional response set off by nothing more than a word, a tone of voice, a look, or even a memory. Unless we develop a new default setting—**a new habit**—it's hard to step back and say to ourselves, *I wonder what's really going on here.*

Sometimes when we ask, *What's going on?* we aren't really feeling curious; rather, we are fearful, defensive, or morally outraged. We've seen this occur when the unthinkable happens, as it did in September 2008, when the banking system of the United States, and in many countries around the world, crumbled. The dramatic impact on stock markets threatened the future of many savings accounts, pensions, jobs, businesses, and dreams. The United States and the world watched expectantly, believing that a proposed $700 billion government bailout bill would stabilize the rapidly spreading panic that was triggering a freeze of the credit markets. Millions of American voters, taxpayers, and citizens made it known they didn't want lawmakers to make such a rash decision. *Not so fast! We don't trust you. How do we know this bailout will work?* they wrote in e-mails, demanded on radio talk programs and blogs, and even protested in the streets. Others wondered what was taking so long to act.

And people were angry, understandably wanting to know, *How did this happen? Who's responsible? Who will pay? What about me?* This form of situational anger is a clue that something is wrong.

We can be more effective if we use anger as a stepping-stone to insight rather than as a springboard for action. Anger can lead us to insight if we can accept it and then activate our curiosity to effectively examine the cause. It would be months before financial experts would begin to acknowledge that in their rush to keep the financial crisis from escalating beyond control, they didn't know what they didn't know. As Jeffrey Sonnenfeld, a professor at Yale School of Management, pointed out shortly after global financial services firm Lehman Brothers filed the largest bankruptcy petition in U.S. history, "No one could have dreamed that it would have gotten this bad, and now that it is, no one is completely certain which choices were right and which were wrong."[4]

How Do I Interrupt an Emotional Hijacking and Make Smarter Choices?

Here's the challenge we face when pressed to respond: unless we can quickly harness our emotional reactions, we might choose the least effective solution *and* solve the wrong problem or miss a hidden opportunity.[5] As one successful executive explained, "I've learned that it is invaluable to have someone you can go to, to vent, because anger is real. It's just not the state of mind in which you want to formulate your response." The Get Curious Not Furious approach provides ways to:

1. Interrupt the rush to react (Pause)
2. Emotionally disengage from what's going on (Suspend Reaction)
3. Get curious; check assumptions and "facts" (Suspend Judgment)
4. Regain control of a situation or control of yourself (Shift to the Right Gear)
5. Make a more informed choice (Move Ahead)

Choosing to be curious allows you to tap into your communication intelligence. Then you can quickly explore what's beneath the surface of what you *think* you know to be true. That's where we find the executive coach and her angry client, George, whose story began in Part One.

Who Does He Think He Is? (Part 2)

Interrupt an emotional hijacking to make smarter choices.

It takes a clear head to maneuver appropriately when it looks like your authority is being undermined. As we'll see in this story, careers can be made or broken in minutes—with a phone call or the click of a mouse.

∞

George was ranting: "How dare John send that e-mail to my team? John was way out of line to think that he had the authority to award a no-bid contract to the vendor they'd used when John was running the show. I just want to blast him."

Having learned the Power of Pause methods, the coach took a moment to reflect, then quickly focused on two things to help her client achieve control. She thought to herself *(1) George thinks that showing anger is the way to show that he is in charge,* and *(2) George's objective should be to handle the people issues of this rapidly growing multimillion-dollar division better than John did when he ran it.*

The coach acknowledged George's anger, saying, "George, you have every right to be angry. It sounds like you feel outmaneuvered and manipulated. To you, it looks like John is trying to do your job and acts like he's in charge."

She then focused George by asking, "What's your objective?"

Without hesitating he responded, "That's easy: to have control and be treated like a leader—not to feel weak and have someone do an end run around me."

To encourage George not to react too quickly to his situation, the coach said, "Let's step back and wonder what we don't know is going on for *John* in this situation."

She questioned whether John had a personal reason for awarding the contract to his old friend. The few minutes it took George to speculate about this possibility gave his anger a breather. He relaxed, laughed, and then said that she could be right; factors other than doing an "end-run" around him might be at work. This helped him shift gears to hear the questions his coach asked that he hadn't thought to ask himself—he regained presence of mind. These were her questions:

1. What *don't we know* that may have motivated John to make the no-bid decision?
2. What kind of pressure might John be under that has *nothing to do with you?*
3. What *other* factors could lead John to think that giving this big contract out to the vendor he'd used when he was in charge would be a good idea?

Instead of blasting John in a return e-mail, George was able to imagine how hard it might be for the former boss to let go of his old authority. That thought had never occurred to him. Then he wrote John, "Let's examine all the variables in making this decision. Here are my thoughts. I'd like to learn more about yours." Unlike John, he did not copy anyone else on the e-mail; he was attempting to work with John on a decision that George previously thought was his alone to make.

George also realized that although John hadn't told him why he thought staying with the current vendor was the right thing to do, George himself hadn't let anyone know he'd made his own decision—to put the contracts out to bid. The two men had something in common: neither thought it was important to involve his team in an important decision. George learned there was value in getting team members involved.

The turning point for George came when he understood that when you get angry, you give away your power and control. He had never thought about it that way; he thought getting angry was a way to show he was powerful. In the end, a leader who thought he needed to succeed by command and control

regained his self-control and his ability to lead by involving people. His coach got him to understand a critical point: **you can't
be an effective leader if you are out of control with anger.**

Putting Ideas to Work

- What up-front agreements could you put in place to avoid
  a misunderstanding over authority? For example, several
  clients teach employees to use rephrasing and the Get
  Curious Not Furious approach at the first sign of a misunderstanding, and not to wait until a situation has become
  intolerable.
- How could you use a paraphrased version of the three
  questions the coach posed to her client to help yourself or
  someone else shift gears when he's angry?

  1. What *don't you know* that may have motivated the
     other person's actions?
  2. What kind of pressure might the other person be under
     that has *nothing to do with you*?
  3. What factors could lead the other person to believe
     that her idea is right?

Why Are So Many of Us Working with Our Fuses Lit and Ready to Blow?

It's easy to be triggered in these high-speed, pressurized times.
Before we know it, we're in the middle of a misunderstanding,

playing offense or defense. We're dealing with outraged customers, or we're fending off drive-by e-mails that can trigger damaging chain reactions.

There's nothing new about how aggravating it can be to feel misunderstood or to misunderstand someone else. **What's new is the speed with which our misunderstanding can happen and then be broadcast beyond recall or our control**. Although advances in technology make it easier and faster to communicate, they also make it easier to miscommunicate. We're at a higher risk of paying the price of snap judgments. Let's look at some of the research.

❖ *Rising stress levels lower effectiveness.* Increased stress affects our ability to process information. Stress can sap our capacity and will to do our best work. Reports from around the world indicate that stress-related symptoms including irritability, anger, nervousness, insomnia, and lack of motivation are on the rise.

❖ *Time urgency impatience syndrome.* There are other factors that can lower our threshold for understanding and affect our health. One of them is impatience. Researchers at Northwestern University in Evanston, Illinois, studied the relationship between living at a "hurry up" pace of life and the significantly increased chance of having high blood pressure. In a fifteen-year study of young adults (ages eighteen to thirty) published in the *Journal of the American Medical Association*, participants were asked to rate their tolerance for waiting or being pressed for time—a pattern of behavior known as "time urgency impatience." The lead author, Lijing L. Yan of Northwestern, explained,

"In general, the stronger the feelings of impatience and time pressure, the higher the risk of developing hypertension in the long term." For some, the impatience meter starts running when we hit the elevator button. As ABC News reported one evening, over the years, designers at the Otis Elevator Company have discovered that we're running out of patience. Their studies show that "in big cities the average person waiting for an elevator starts to get anxious in less than 30 seconds. A minute is considered an eternity."[6]

We are built for speed. As author Malcolm Gladwell reported in his book *Blink*, our agile, "thin-slicing" brain allows us to quickly, often unconsciously, process input and make snap decisions about what we're hearing, seeing, or sensing. He explains, "There's a wonderful phrase in psychology—"the power of thin slicing"—which says that as human beings we are capable of making sense of situations based on the thinnest slice of experience."[7] This is especially true if we are (or think we are) experts in that particular topic or recognize a pattern. His research also reveals that unless we pause for a beat or two, at times we're likely to be guided by our prejudices and stereotypes.

We're suffering from e-mail apnea. Linda Stone, an adviser for the Pew Internet and American Life Project and a former senior executive at Apple Computers and Microsoft, has identified another phenomenon that explains why it's so easy to get caught up in the trip wires of electronic misunderstandings, attacks, and countermeasures. She observed that when people were e-mailing one another, they were holding their breath. She interviewed researchers at the National Institutes of Health as well as other experts and physicians, who confirmed that breath holding and shallow breathing had an impact on the nervous system. What's intriguing about her discovery is the connection she identifies between holding our breath and the urge to react fast because our brain shifts into a fight-or-flight mode. She called this phenomenon e-mail apnea.[8]

➷ *It's harder to slow down.* Our tolerance, attention spans, and fuses are also affected by the fact that more and more of us are working longer days, skipping meals, and taking shorter vacations, if we take them at all.

➷ *We've lost the "human moment."* Two leading experts in attention deficit disorder, Dr. John Ratey and Dr. Edward Hallowell, identified environmental factors that may be promoting attention deficit problems in the general population. In their book, *Delivered from Distraction*, Hallowell explains that technology has infiltrated so many intimate corners of our lives that it is diminishing our ability to communicate: "Television, cell phones, Walkmen, the Internet, video games, Game Boys, faxes, e-mails, Black Berries and all the rest of the electronic means and devices we love have wound their way so possessively into our lives that we spend less and less time with one another face-to-face. The electronic moment is supplanting what I call the human moment. Without meaning to, we are losing touch with one another."[9]

Given these environmentally induced tendencies for us to misunderstand one another and set off our fight-or-flight responses, here's a question to ask ourselves: *Why am I wasting*

*time defending myself or blaming others when I'm in the grip
of a misunderstanding? It may be my fault, it may be their
fault, but it really doesn't matter.* **Blame isn't the avenue to
understanding. We have to change our mindset.**

"Missed Understandings" Set Off Chain Reactions

Think about the last time you felt misunderstood. *You* knew
exactly what you meant when you spoke to someone, sent
that note, or left that voice mail or text message. If you're like
most of us, it wasn't the first time you felt misinterpreted.
Maybe one person was distracted. Another person expected
you to say something else, or he had a reaction to what you
said and started rehearsing a response. There could be many
other reasons why what you said didn't come through as you
meant it, including your own unrecognized ambivalence.
Then again, most people rarely wonder about what you
didn't say. We are misunderstood more than we realize. One
way to keep yourself from taking a communication snafu
personally is to call it a "missed understanding" to simply
remind yourself that something was missed.

To be fair, let's put the shoe on the other foot (so that it's
harder to take it personally when it happens to you). When
was the last time you misunderstood someone—a colleague,
client, prospective customer, vendor, patient, boss, student,
spouse, stranger, or friend? How do you think that person
felt when her words or her actions were misinterpreted even
when she thought she was being perfectly clear?

POWER OF PAUSE PRACTICE #2:
Be Aware of Your Filters (and Theirs)

One way to think of what you are doing while you process the many inputs you receive is to think of yourself as having conversations—with yourself! Internal conversations act like filters, affecting how much we hear and how we react to it. They shape our interpretations and what we think we heard someone say. For example, *Wall Street Journal* reporter Jonathan Clements writes about the phenomenon of confirmation bias. This concept addresses why the more you are invested in an idea or a decision, the more you seek information that confirms your viewpoint, *without realizing that you are screening out alternative data.*[10]

Whether you are on the phone with a customer or in a room full of people at a meeting, imagine them "listening" while filtering out meaning and content. As the following list shows, they are carrying on internal conversations and *also* texting, computing, videoconferencing, and e-mailing. The challenge is to learn how to communicate well *in spite of* what's happening around you.

While someone else is speaking, our minds are busy simultaneously sorting through any number of reactions:

Filters Affect What We *Think* We See, Hear, and Sense

1. **Assuming:** I know what you are going to say. (Mind checks out)
2. **Reacting to expectations:** That's not what I expected you to say. (Mind reacts)
3. **Solving:** I wish you'd finish; I have the answer [an idea]. (Mind impatient)
4. **Taking it personally:** I don't like [respect] you. (Mind invalidates)
5. **Questioning:** I don't understand what you're saying. (Mind uncomfortable)
6. **Disagreeing:** I don't agree with what you are saying. (Mind wants to argue)
7. **Agreeing:** I agree; that's what I think. (Mind says, "Got it, let's move on")
8. **Planning:** I've got another appointment. (Mind preparing for what's next)
9. **Processing prior events:** I can't focus on this right now. (Mind not present)
10. **Juggling:** When's lunch? What can I do about my father's illness? (Mind stressed)

Figure 4.1. Filters Reduce Your Attention Span

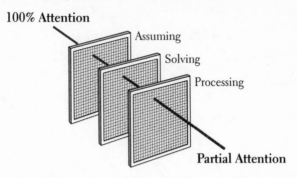

Other factors that can cause us to tune out include reacting to another person's accent, look, gender, presentation skills, tone of voice, and credentials (or lack of them).[11]

Once you recognize how automatically your brain filters communication, you can appreciate the importance of confirming your *interpretation* of what you think someone said and meant. You can't turn the filters off completely, but you can develop the awareness to catch yourself when your attention is distracted by your internal reactions. **Then you will be less likely to take it personally** when someone misses something *you* said. And you won't waste time being defensive when someone points out, as you can see in Figure 4.1, that while your mind was busy assuming, solving, or processing, your attention drifted off and you misinterpreted what *she* meant.

As you saw in the list of filters, when you are busy interpreting someone's communications, you can easily be distracted by internal conversations. It's nearly impossible to focus 100 percent of your attention on what the person is attempting to convey. Naturally this opens the door for missed understandings.

CHAPTER 5

GET A REALITY CHECK

SAVE TIME, MONEY, AND RELATIONSHIPS

Considering the information we looked at in Chapter Four, is it any wonder that 70 to 80 percent of what someone communicates isn't understood or remembered?[1] Yes, it's frustrating and it wastes time and offends people, which is costly and senseless. However, this awareness gives you a reality check—and makes it all the more important to use communication intelligence tools and attitudes to prevent or handle missed understandings. Let's look at some ways to save time and to be more effective and less stressed by not taking misunderstandings so personally.

POWER OF PAUSE PRACTICE #3:
Give the Benefit of the Doubt

If we want to get ahead in a high-performance workplace, why not start by automatically giving others the benefit of the doubt?

Even if it's just for a few minutes, as we start to unravel a problem, this could give us the winning edge in the end. Instead of jumping to a conclusion, we'd be able to consider that maybe something got lost in translation or allow ourselves or others a chance to save face. In other instances we learn that we don't know the whole story of what drives someone's behavior. For example, as a coach and business consultant, I've worked with many successful professionals with attention deficit disorder whose intentions and behavior are often misunderstood. That's one reason why I urge you to give **anyone** the momentary benefit of the doubt and use the Power of Pause practices to discern—without judging people—what's motivating their behavior.

POWER OF PAUSE PRACTICE #4:
Stop Putting Deposits in Your Resentment Bank Account

There are times when we unconsciously put "deposits" in what I call our Resentment Bank Account, and they are earning interest, ready to fund our overreaction to someone when we least expect it. If something you said or did bothered me, and I never told you about it because it wasn't worth the effort or the risk, it would become a deposit in my Resentment Bank Account and begin earning interest. Now there's a good chance that I'm less likely to care about making the effort to understand you. I may even go out of my way to undermine or avoid you. This "banked" memory can fester, raising my stress level and eroding our relationship. One day I'll blow up at you or at some other unsuspecting soul because I'm more sick and tired of stuffing my resentment than I realize. (We look more at this concept in Part Three.)

•••

In this next story, you'll see the results that a pause and a few minutes of curiosity, combined with giving the benefit of the doubt, produced for a company's bottom line and for its culture.

It's Not About the Name Tags!

How do you get employees to listen to you when there's a lot at stake and you think that what they're doing is wrong?

Any day now, the rating inspectors will show up to determine whether the hotel's service merits raising its Three Diamond status to a Four Diamond rating. The higher rating is expected to increase revenues by attracting higher-income customers. Every employee has been told to provide "warm, friendly personal service to the guests." However, the hotel has a problem: a number of the employees keep showing up at work without their brand-new, official brass name-tag pins. Others, who wear their name tags, are seen looking down at the carpet when they pass guests in the hallways of the hotel. Neither behavior is going to score the points the hotel needs if it's to be awarded that coveted rating. Watch what happens when the hotel managers shift from assumption-driven reactions to offering their staff the benefit of the doubt.

First, the hotel managers decided they just needed to remind all the employees about the new rule by telling them, "As you

---

know, our new policy is that you must wear name badges, look the guests in the eye as you pass them, and offer a greeting or ask them, 'How is your stay?' "

Nothing changed.

Then managers decided to penalize people if they were found without their name tags. That didn't work either.

When pressed to explain why they weren't following the policies, employees said that the name tag pins put holes in the uniforms or that the name tags fell off. Management thought they'd solved the problem when they decided to buy magnetic name badges and officially reprimand employees who didn't comply.

When I heard about this plan, I asked the general manager whether I could spend a few moments with some of the staff. Even though she was ready to take action, having been convinced by her managers that they'd identified the problem, she was also willing to be curious. She didn't want to waste time and resources solving the wrong problem, so she gave me permission to talk to the employees. I suspected that we didn't know the whole story behind why employees—who had never worn name tags before—were refusing to wear them. Our dialogue was brief and revealing as I rephrased what I thought *and* what I sensed the employees were trying to say:

Staff: We're worried about talking to the guests.
(*Before I responded, I was wondering what they meant by the word "worried." So I took a guess; I wasn't concerned about being wrong because most people will understand you are just trying to help them, and they will correct you.*)
Me: So it sounds like you are concerned that you might not know how to help the guests if they ask you for something.
Staff: Yes, and you need to understand, we work in maintenance or housekeeping or at the bell stand or in room service.
(*I wasn't as sure of what I sensed they were saying with that comment, so I let them know of my uncertainty.*)

74

Me: Let me see if I'm getting the picture. You'd like to help a guest because you care, but you aren't sure what to do if they ask you to help them with something that you're not trained to do.
Staff: Well, sort of but not really—the problem is that we don't know who to go to in management to get an answer for the guests.
Me: Oh, so if I get what you're saying, you're worried about how you're supposed to know the answers to questions that people from other departments handle.

More came out in the conversation as I continued to pause and rephrase. As a result, we discovered that:

- Departments were meeting weekly to monitor improvement and address problems, so everyone was "on guard" for what could go wrong.
- When something went wrong—with a booking, room cleanliness, a special event, or room service—there was a lot of blame going around among the department heads, who would quickly present "evidence" that another department was at fault.
- This "blame game" made the employees even less willing to risk interacting with a guest or even a colleague who needed their help.

Of course the problem wasn't the name tags!
The problem was that employees were scared that if a guest asked them to do something or complained about something, the guest would know their name. They'd never had to wear name badges before, and now they felt exposed if something went wrong. They didn't want to be blamed for something that wasn't their fault. Had the hotel management continued to try to get the employees to cooperate by enforcing the rules, they would have missed the opportunity to do what author Patrick Lencioni teaches so well in his books *Silos, Politics and*

Turf Wars and *The Five Dysfunctions of a Team:* they would have missed the real cause of the problem, which was that each department was only taking care of its own turf.

Return on Investment
Working with the hotel managers, we initiated a Stop the Blame campaign and held a managers' retreat where everyone learned skills to help them have timely, open-minded, courageous conversations and to stop taking things so personally. The result? Managers were able to solve problems more quickly and to trust one another. They started visiting the other departments' meetings to get to know the staff and to explain how to refer guests to them. Not only did the hotel win their Four Diamond rating, its staff meetings also stopped being dominated by the blame game. Suddenly this group of individuals started coming together as a real team.

What did the general manager have to do to get this return on her investment in a few minutes of rephrasing by a consultant? She had to set aside what she and others previously assumed was an "obvious" lack of commitment by employees. She was willing to pause and get curious just long enough to learn that rephrasing and listening for a few moments were actions that spoke louder than words. Rephrasing is now a routine practice at this hotel, which has continued to maintain its high ratings and remain profitable during challenging times for the hotel industry.

∞

POWER OF PAUSE PRACTICE #5:
Use Rephrasing as a Twenty-First-Century Risk Management Tool

Given the speed with which incorrect assumptions and demand-driven decisions can boomerang on us today, rephrasing becomes much more than a communication technique. It becomes a profit-generating, time-saving, trust-building risk management practice.

In its most basic form, rephrasing is reformulating (putting into your own words) what you think someone meant. You build trust by revealing how you "filtered" that person's communication and by giving him a chance to confirm or clarify what you interpreted. This is a habit worth developing. It's a modest up-front investment that saves time in the end and produces better decisions. It's a powerful pause.

Showing your intention to understand the meaning behind someone's communication, rather than to prove that you are right, makes it easier for someone to reveal *more* than she initially said. She is more likely to trust you when you are first willing to reveal, through rephrasing, how you filtered her communication, giving her a chance to fill in what so often gets lost in translation.

For years, colleagues, clients, and I have noticed that although many people read books on communication or take workshops that teach rephrasing, they say that they don't feel comfortable applying what they've learned. In contrast, people who have learned the Power of Pause rephrasing framework report that it becomes second nature. My field research has shown that to make rephrasing part of your leadership DNA, it takes (1) presence of mind (pause), (2) an extra dimension of humility to risk revealing your interpretation of another person's communication, and (3) consistent practice. You begin to turn this practice into an effective habit by asking yourself two quick questions:

1. Is there something I (or the other person) might be assuming, filtering, reacting to, or missing?

2. Is this an opportunity to pause, get curious, and, while I'm in the "neutral zone," stick my neck out to show not how much I know but how much I care to understand?

"High touch" is a phrase *Megatrends* author John Naisbett coined in the 1980s to signify the need for humanizing outreach to counterbalance increased mechanization.[2] Rephrasing restores "high touch" in today's high-tech, high-speed, high-performance workplace. You can use rephrasing with e-mail, telephone exchanges, conference calls, and video conferences, one-on-one or in a group. (If you are hesitant about using rephrasing, think it will take too much time, or are concerned that you might get it wrong, these are valid concerns, and we'll deal with them in the Tips and *Yeah, buts* section for Part Two.)

Before rephrasing what you think someone meant by what he said or wrote, it is crucial that you have the right mindset: one of curiosity. Your words and actions must reflect your attitude. This means that you will need the discipline to suspend disbelief and set aside assumptions. As you will see in the next chapter, that's where cultivating curiosity comes into play.

CHAPTER 6

WHAT *IS* CURIOSITY?

The voyage of discovery lies not in seeking new
vistas but in having new eyes. We need to learn
to see with new eyes.

—MARCEL PROUST

W hat if we could learn to see with new eyes?
Curiosity is a state of mind that provides access
to communication intelligence. When we are
curious, we're willing to set aside our need to be right. We're
committed to something more than just the facts. We're willing to be wrong, or to learn something and use it to redirect
our thinking and our actions. When we're curious, we're
open to possibilities, and it is this mindset that allows us to
seek genuine understanding.

POWER OF PAUSE PRACTICE #6:
Use the Get Curious Not Furious Approach

These days it's not that easy to access a sense of curiosity when
emotions are running high, you feel outranked, or you're

pressed for a decision. That's why I've developed several cues to alert you to how curious you *or others* may be at a given moment. This Curiosity Cues Checklist (see page 83) gives you a fast way to pause and consider your most effective response—given your goals, the time you have, and your need for insight. Take a moment to think about a current or past situation and use the checklist to weigh your (or someone else's) level of curiosity. You'll be able to make a timely U-turn when confronting a closed mind or a reaction zone.

Enhance Innovation

Curiosity isn't only important as a means to slow down your urge to react. It's also a state of mind that can create a new generation of ideas. It's not uncommon to feel pulled in two directions on the job: there's the pressure to get the work done right and fast; there's also pressure to innovate. Author Dawna Markova is known for her research on learning and perception. In a *New York Times* interview, she emphasizes, "The first thing needed for innovation is a fascination with wonder. But we are taught instead to 'decide.'"[1]

How *do* you resist the pressure to act? Give yourself permission to pause. In that moment, you have a choice to explore a possibility, which could take you in an entirely different direction.

Life is full of edits. We edit what we say, what we write, what we think, what we share. We edit when we pull a punch in conversation or curb our thoughts lest we offend someone. Think of any difficult conversation you've had, and you can think of edits that you made. When you edit, you make choices and exercise decisions that determine what comes next.

Countless fields now require people to process tremendous amounts of information, whether they are working in health care or government or finance or news gathering. Peter Shaplen is an award-winning broadcast journalist, business owner, and former news director who has dealt with deadline-driven decisions most of his life. In this reflection, he shares a lesson about the risks he took early in his career as a video producer. He wrestled with the dilemma of creativity versus speed when faced with choosing which frames of video, when edited together, would best tell a story. Today, he echoes Markova's cautionary plea to make room for possibilities.

Decide, Decide, Decide!

∾ You don't get a lot of previews in life today. You just decide, decide, decide!

Thirty years ago, when video editing was in its infancy, the machines were imperfect. The editor would set the in-point of an edit, where they wanted something to begin, and the out cue, or where they wanted that shot to end. But often it seemed even though the editor had been very precise, once the red edit button was hit, the final product was not what had been marked. The machine had "slipped," and the edit marks—the in and the out—were ever so slightly different and wrong from what was intended. You'd have to start the process all over again.

There was an option. Instead of the red edit button which, once hit, committed everyone to that edit, good or bad, right or wrong, there was a white "preview" edit button. This would allow you a glimpse of what the machine thought you wanted and would create.

Today we often find ourselves being trigger-happy. Pressed for time or infused with a sense of our own value or responsibilities, we think we know what to do or say. Or we don't think we have a choice. Then there are the times when we go off half-cocked on issues where we feel righteous. We don't think of the consequences.

By pausing I can ask myself, *Is it worthy of my time, my thought, or me?* Pausing gives me the chance to make a choice. It gives me my power back—over myself.

Here is a quote from Henry David Thoreau that inspired me while I was researching the nature of curiosity:

It is an important epoch when a man who has always lived on the east side of a mountain and seen it in the west, travels round and sees it in the east.

An Ounce of Prevention Is Worth a Pound of Cure

Because it is increasingly likely that we can misunderstand or be misunderstood, why not take responsibility to mitigate that risk?

Curiosity Cues Checklist

Values Knowing	Values Learning
Lower Chance of Being Curious	Higher Chance of Being Curious
☐ Am I focused on facts as *the* truth? (Are they focused on facts as *the* truth?)	☐ Do we acknowledge that facts might not tell the whole story?
☐ Is my mind made up? (Are their minds made up?)	☐ Do we recognize that another way is possible?
☐ Is my experience driving decisions? (Are their experiences driving decisions?)	☐ Do we stay open to consider others' experience?
☐ Am I invested in having my expectations met? (Are they invested in having their expectations met?)	☐ Are we intrigued to consider the unexpected?
☐ Do I value being right, and am I usually right? (Do they value being right, and are they usually right?)	☐ Do we value alternative routes?
☐ Do I believe that I communicated clearly? (Do they feel their communication was crystal clear?)	☐ Are we open to the possibility of a "missed understanding" on our part or on theirs?

You can reduce your chances of becoming tangled up in time-wasting misunderstandings by adopting a seamless three-step habit to mentally shift gears: (1) pause, to shift to neutral; (2) use the Get Curious Not Furious process, to suspend your assumptions and reactions; and (3) rephrase, to reveal the underlying issues and discover a more effective solution.

It's easier than you think to shift to this way of responding instead of reacting.

One way to adopt a new habit—even if you're not sure it's right for you yet—is to think about a similar habit you have that produces a positive result. For example, when someone gives you a telephone number, what's the first thing you automatically do? You repeat it. After hearing it, you repeat what you think the person said. He might need to correct a mistake or reconsider and give you additional ways to reach him, making your job easier in the end.

Think of it this way: numbers don't have shades of meaning. Yet we double-check because we know it's easy to transpose a number or hear it incorrectly. In conversations and other verbal interchanges, it's even more important to do a "meaning check" by inserting a pause and at least one rephrase. As you saw earlier, like it or not, today more than ever, we filter how we interpret communication. It's important to remember: **meaning isn't in the words; it is in how you interpret the words.**

An attitude of curiosity enables you to proceed with an open mind. Here is one example of how you can put this to work. We learned earlier that Linda Stone's research suggests that because our brain is primed for action, we're wired to fight or flee when we're exchanging e-mails. In contrast, if you have learned to pause, to get curious, and to rephrase when you feel "hit" by e-mails, you realize you have a choice in how to respond.

Learning to suspend your automatic response, like the early stage of forming any new habit, starts with the

afterthought of awareness. This stage reminds me of the television commercial for the vegetable drink, V8. The ad shows
people, after having had something else (presumably less
healthy) to drink, thinking to themselves, *I could have had a
V8!* It's important to remember that at first, when we're trying
to develop a new habit, we're still going to forget to pause—
and at that point we have our "I coulda" afterthought. So the
next time you are tempted to react automatically to the push
of high-speed communication, the commercial reminder in
your head might sound like, *I could have paused and gotten
curious.*

The 3 A's of Behavior Change

Motivating people to listen, to learn, and to rethink problems and solutions was a topic of research when I worked
for Westinghouse Broadcasting as a director of editorials
and communications. For nine years—through editorials,
public service, and cause-related marketing programs—I was
responsible for leading national and statewide initiatives in
complicated behavior change. We educated and inspired the
public and officials to adopt new habits that had been previously unthinkable. These included the Designated Driver
program, to motivate people to stop drinking and driving; the
For Kids' Sake and *Time to Care* campaigns, to help people
rethink their responsibilities in addressing the unmet needs
of children and the public; persuading people to donate
organs, to save a life; and educating them about important

ways to prevent AIDS. I've witnessed time and again the shift from apathy to awareness to action; it is the process of a new habit forming. I call it the **3 A's of Behavior Change:**

Apathy → Awareness → Action

Researching and implementing these initiatives confirmed my perception: **to inspire people to change their behavior, you cannot blame or shame them for what they believe or what they have done in the past.** Instead, you have to give people a way to move away from their opinion, or their apathy, to an awareness of information that is new or was previously rejected. You then give them small steps to take to move from awareness to action. If you use this 3 A's approach to motivating behavior change, people tend to adopt a new frame of mind because they do not feel judged when they are informed about a new alternative. This awareness-raising approach enables people to act in their own self-interest and in the interest of others without triggering their defensiveness. These field-tested insights are one reason why the principles and practices in this book work. They reflect an appreciation of how to lower resistance to change.

As you'll see in the remaining chapters of Part Two, developing the habit of shifting into the "curiosity gear" also opens the door to having a less judgmental mind and reduces the stress of coming to terms with change. That frame of mind fosters innovation, better decisions, and better teamwork on behalf of colleagues *and* customers.

CHAPTER 7

HAVE YOU BEEN CAUGHT IN A DECISION-MAKING SPEED TRAP?

We've addressed reactions driven by emotions. Now let's shift gears to talk about times when we're making decisions and our emotions haven't been hijacked, but our brains are on fast-forward just the same. We're relying on experience and the urge to be immediately effective.

Our tendency to develop our own mental decision-making maps is described by Dr. Jerome Groopman in his book *How Doctors Think.* He says he wrote the book because he was disturbed and curious about the reports of increasing rates of medical errors. He explains that many errors stem more from how doctors think than from problems with technology. Relying on decades of research in cognitive psychology, Groopman describes three "habits of the mind" that doctors use to enable them to make snap judgments. Groopman explains that this mental sorting can reduce the time it takes for them to make a diagnosis from twenty minutes to twenty seconds, but it can also produce cognitive traps and mistakes.

87

For instance, one of the snap decision-making habits he discusses is *anchoring*: "Confirming what you expect to find by selectively accepting or ignoring information. The person doesn't consider multiple possibilities but quickly and firmly latches onto a single one, sure that he has thrown his anchor down just where he needs to be."[1]

For an example of anchoring in the business world, imagine you are the owner of a successful heating and cooling business. You have spent two years with a prospective customer evaluating the most efficient options to replace a twenty-five-year-old heating system. You are meeting with the homeowner to go over the details of this expensive installation. You've told her twice that there is no way to run a heating duct into the unheated room that she wants to use year-round as an office in her small home. On previous visits, you quickly assessed what you always see in houses like this one with a floor that looks as if it's on a slab foundation. On this last visit, she asks you once again, "Isn't there *any* way to heat this room?"

Wait a minute, you say to yourself. *I can't believe I didn't see this the first two times: it's not on a slab; it's just that there's no crawl space. Of course we can run a duct in there. Piece of cake. Why didn't I see it?*

You didn't see it because of the anchoring phenomenon. Your mind was already "attached" to what you expected to see.

You've probably experienced a similar blind spot yourself, whether you were the customer or the person trying to help someone else. Doctors aren't the only ones reaching for familiar clues to satisfy the need for instant answers, and of course, sometimes it is these very mechanisms for decision making that can help save the day. But as we've seen, they can also lead us down the wrong path. Like doctors, we can come to the wrong snap conclusion that prematurely rules out the very possibilities that could lead to a better solution. A variation of coming to snap conclusions happens when you attempt to solve a problem that is not the real problem, as we saw in the earlier story about the hotel employees' refusal to wear nametags. There's an ancient Zen saying: *Problems are rarely solved at the level they are first expressed.*

As you'll see in the rest of this chapter, none of us has time to waste solving the wrong problem. That's why taking a few minutes to clarify and confirm what you think someone means saves you time and effort. It also ensures that you don't walk away from a problem thinking that it's solved, when all you may have done is address the "presenting" issue at the surface.

Why Is It So Hard to Give or Get Customer Service Today?

Here's the problem: by the time customers talk to a service representative, they are often already upset. Something didn't turn out the way they expected. (Remember, most upsets are the result of a misunderstood or unexpressed expectation.) You could say that they are "anger waiting to happen." Customer service expert Kirk Kazanjian has found that "if you're not properly trained in how to turn around an angry customer, you may get angry yourself."[2]

Unfortunately, unless the customer has paused, gotten curious, and set aside her assumptions, both of you acceler-ate and move into the high-speed "furious" lane. That's why it's so important—even a competitive advantage—for you to be able to pause to get genuinely curious about what's going on for her.

If you are the customer service responder who's trying to help, it's probably not your fault that something went wrong. However, you can connect much more effectively if you take a moment to appreciate why customers may be saying to themselves, *Can you blame me for being so angry?* Recall the cycle of a reaction illustrated in Figures I.1 and 2.1: the minute something happens, there is a chain reaction. That's why customers may feel entitled to be mad, to get a quick resolution, or to go to the top for a straight answer. This train of thought can come into play whether your customer is a patient, taxpayer, student, volunteer, manager, colleague, or the CEO.

As sociologist Charles Tilly writes in his book *Credit and Blame*, the human habit of trying to affix blame when something goes wrong is apparently part of our "All-Purpose Justice Detector."[3] The last thing customers want to hear is that the problem is their fault and nothing can be done—even if that's true. This is one of those times that telling someone, "This must be so frustrating for you; let's see what we can do to find out what's going on," is a powerful first step toward a winning solution.[4]

•••

In the next two stories, we'll learn how to turn a disappointed customer into a loyal fan and how to hold on to a customer who has one foot out the door, while also holding on to your profit margin.

#1 When You Deliver Beyond Expectations
How do you start a conversation that doesn't begin with who's to blame?

There are times when a customer believes he's done everything right, but something has gone terribly wrong. It takes presence of mind for a customer service agent to appreciate the caller's discomfort and quickly sort through the facts while keeping options open for a positive resolution.

It was almost Christmas. The unimaginable had happened. With great anticipation, loyal Amazon.com customer and *New York Times* financial columnist Joe Nocera had ordered the hottest new PlayStation 3 video game player for his son. When the gift was delivered to his New York City apartment building, it was left with a neighbor, who signed for the package and left it in a public hallway for Nocera to pick up. As you might guess, it wasn't there when he went to get it. Was all lost? Here's what happened next.

Nocera called Amazon and spoke to the customer service agent. He didn't think there was a chance that Amazon would send him a replacement. To his astonishment, as he put it, "the customer service guy didn't even blink." In minutes, after confirming the details of his story, the agent offered to send him a replacement at no cost, not even for shipping! Were his expectations unreasonable? Yes, *very* unreasonable, by his own admission.

What did Amazon gain? One raving, loyal fan who also got curious enough to check how well the company's stock was doing. Nocera suspected that Amazon might be struggling, having become just one of many Internet retailers after its earlier high-flying days, before the Internet bubble burst.

91

To his surprise, Amazon's stock was up 140 percent over the prior year. He asked several financial analysts why the stock was doing so well. Although they had their own answers, here's what Nocera wrote in his front-page column for the *New York Times* business section: "But I couldn't help wondering if maybe there wasn't something else at play here, something Wall Street never seems to take very seriously. Maybe, just maybe, taking care of customers is something worth doing when you are trying to create a lasting company. Maybe it's the best way to build a business even if it comes at the expense of short-term results."[5]

∞

#2 Oh No, Here We Go: Suspending the Urge to Put Up Defenses

How do you keep new customers from leaving in tight economic times and feel good about the special terms you agree to offer them?

That's what Sally Woodson, the codirector of a successful Music Together® early childhood music program in New York City, faced one day when the phone rang.

∞

I was in the office about a week after our fall semester began, and got a phone call from a mom who wanted to pull out of the program and get a refund. My first reaction was, "Oh no, here we go . . . She's unhappy because her child is the youngest in the class. Or she found out that her friends were all doing some other class, which she wanted to do with them instead."

The first words out of my mouth were *almost* "We don't allow refunds after class begins."

Instead, I paused, took a breath, and got curious. I asked the mom if she was unhappy with the class and if so, why. She said, "Oh, it's just not working out."

As we kept talking (she wasn't terribly forthcoming at first), I asked her if she was familiar with Music Together and how our classes worked. She then told me that she had taken the program at one of our affiliates in another city and loved it. This made me *really* curious.

When I asked her if she and her child had fun in our class, she said, "Yes." I asked her when she had moved to the city, and she said they had just gotten here this summer. As she spoke further, she talked about the "sticker shock" that she and her husband were experiencing. I said that I had felt the same way when I had moved from the Midwest.

Then she opened up and said that she and her husband were students living here for just a year. Although they had been put in housing on the Upper East Side—so it looked like they had a posh address—they actually had very little money for extras. Once I realized that the problem wasn't the quality of our class, it was about her budget, we were able to work out a price that she could accept. She was thrilled, felt welcomed to a big new city, and I also assured her that we would work with her financially for the entire term that they would be here. We both hung up happy!

Putting Ideas to Work

When you are about to lose a customer, it's hard to pause and put your automatic defenses on hold. Sally is a successful businesswoman dealing with demands on her time, her budget, and her customers. She volunteered that taking several Power of Pause workshops had given her skills to effectively

turn a problem into an opportunity. In her own words, here's
how she applies the practices:

- **Do not jump to conclusions.** My first thoughts about why
  she wanted to pull out were completely wrong.
- **Do not be in a hurry to try to fix things.** Sometimes I'm
  tempted to quickly take care of the unhappy customer.
  That's not something I like to admit, but on days when the
  phone is ringing and ringing, I can start feeling that way.
- **Do really listen!** Not to the words, but to so much more.
  The mom's first words were that the program wasn't working for them. I never would have guessed that it wasn't
  working for them because it was too expensive, seeing as
  they had already signed up and paid! I was trying to listen
  to what was *unsaid*. Pausing and breathing and asking
  questions gave me that opportunity.

CHAPTER 8

WHEN CURIOSITY BECOMES YOUR NEW DEFAULT SETTING

U sing the Get Curious Not Furious methodology can raise your communication intelligence. Instead of being emotionally hijacked or fighting back armed with "the facts," you'll be able to pause long enough to regain self-control and choose a better route to success.

This next case history is about differences in leadership values and management styles. More important, it's about how a senior executive leveraged her curiosity to keep her options open when she found herself on a collision course with a powerful leader in her organization. When these kinds of disagreements happen with people who have decision-making authority over you, you must manage the emotional fallout; otherwise you risk losing the ability to lead your own team.

I Needed to Step Into His Shoes

What do you do when you and your boss don't see eye-to-eye?

It's budget time, and without warning you and your boss discover there's a huge gap separating how you each believe people should be motivated and rewarded. That's what happened to Joyce Elam, executive dean of Florida International University's College of Business Administration, when she was expecting to award well-earned bonuses to her top performers. *As you read this story, I invite you to step into Dean Elam's shoes.*

It's budget time: It's January, and you submit your budget for the coming year, which includes the incentive compensation package that was approved five years ago for your top performers in marketing and recruiting. Under the plan, they could earn up to 50 percent of their salary as a bonus based on the number and quality of students they recruit and retain for the graduate school's business programs.

Your expectations: Your staff had a record year, beating your expectations and turning over more than their fair share of revenues to the university. You are proud of their achievements and are looking forward to rewarding them for their success in a very competitive market for graduate students.

Unexpected change in plans: Two months later, you are surprised when the vice president who oversees university budget decisions contacts you to say there's concern about the "rich" plan. You are asked to modify it by reducing the percentage of their salary as a bonus your employees can earn.

The counteroffer: You meet at length with your boss's top assistant to see what would be acceptable. Working with his staff and the lawyers, you craft a new incentive package that limits bonuses to 30 percent of salary. You have requested that the final decision be made in time to start the new fiscal year, June 30.

Your expectations: You submit your material to the lawyers a month in advance of that deadline. You want the approval in time to give your employees fair notice of something that isn't going to seem fair to them. You don't get the plan back until July, so now you're feeling the pressure because you know your people assume that their compensation program is the same as last year. After working hard on this with your boss's top adviser, you expect the compromise plan will be accepted—just a bit later than you had requested.

Without warning: You receive a brief e-mail stating that your boss, who has the final word on all budgets in the university, will not approve any bonus plan. It is a point blank *no* without an explanation.

Your first reaction: You are stunned. You feel you've negotiated in good faith and done your due diligence. You didn't see this decision coming.

In the past, you would have: Become furious, and enlisted the necessary people in supporting your "evidence" that this decision not only is unfair but also doesn't make sense. You would make the case, "We're going back on our word with our people." You'd point out, "We say we're an entrepreneurial organization, and now we're not being rewarded for being entrepreneurial?" Maybe you could win the battle. Only later would you realize that you had lost the war because you'd gained a reputation for winning that made it look as if you had your own base of financial power and had received special treatment.

Today you pause, again: You meet again with your boss's top assistant. First you explain that you need to vent. He agrees to just listen. Then you tell him your plan to inform the boss in graphic detail about the serious consequences of his decision. Your adviser understands your alarm but warns, "You may be right about the consequences, but a 'threat' approach won't work with him." You decide to take another course.

Before you meet with your boss: You're now able to shift gears to set your anger on hold and explore what you assumed or didn't know. You pause to ask yourself some questions about what might be driving his reaction. That's the frame of mind you are in when you meet with your boss and say, without anger at that moment, "Help me understand what your concerns are about the revised proposal."

The meeting: It quickly becomes obvious to you that even your revised plan makes your boss uncomfortable because it comes at a time of budget cuts and layoffs. He finds it awkward to have some of your people receive such a rich incentive plan. He tells you that the last thing he needs is for the press to print that people are getting 30 percent of their salary in bonuses when the university has already been criticized for faculty and staff layoffs.

Your boss's point of view: He tells you, "It's not just the press coming after us at a bad time. It's that no one else in the organization is paid this way." He asks you whether this type of incentive plan is in place at other universities. You rephrase what you think he's telling you and agree to look into it. You ask, "Is there anything else you can tell me that made you turn our proposal down?"

The big ah-HA! "Yes," he continues, "frankly, I think that it's important that all employees should be treated the same. It's not fair that some other units across the university don't have the opportunity that your unit does to bring in the revenues you can attract. It's not right that your people are getting bonuses at all."

Another reaction—you are surprised again! You can feel a reaction coming, thinking to yourself, *How am I going to deal with this?* In the past you would have gotten defensive and tried to persuade him that your incentive plan was the right way to motivate and reward people in the business school. Given the organization's emphasis on entrepreneurial thinking, you had never considered his more traditional outlook as an overriding budget philosophy. His point of view is an unexpected new data point that's contrary to your map from the business world, where giving special treatment to motivate those who meet their goals is common practice.

Going forward, you innovate: In your follow-up meeting, you'll acknowledge that yours is the only business school you know of that uses such incentive-based compensation. You'll make the case that nonetheless, your team should be rewarded for pioneering an entrepreneurial compensation plan.

What Happened?

The vice president discovered that there was a little-known, university-wide variable compensation plan that allowed for the type of bonus compensation the dean had been seeking. University leaders met to discuss the policy, which imposed no limits on the amount an employee could earn as a bonus. The group voted to continue the compensation policy, but decided to limit bonuses to 10 percent of salary. The dean's team was disappointed, but no one quit, despite the 20 percent drop in their potential earnings. They appreciated that she had made a strong case for them and knew she had originated the initial bonus plan on their behalf.

There's more to the story. Recognizing the limits placed on the university-based sales and marketing position, the dean pioneered a strategic partnership with an outside firm that specializes in working with universities. She hired it to handle the sales and marketing for new initiatives, including an online MBA program. After ten years as dean, Elam decided it was time to expand her interest and skills in developing entrepreneurial ventures to go beyond just the business school to include the university at large. She was appointed dean of a new university-wide unit that will oversee the rapidly expanding Online University as well as other professional development programs.

Lessons Learned

Looking back at this experience, Dean Elam shared these thoughts: "Today I don't see my boss as the enemy in this situation. Years ago, no matter who the boss was, that's how I would have seen it. Today I see him as someone who was struggling against many odds trying to do the best job he could do. We just had a basic disagreement about values, and the way we would manage and motivate people to succeed. It was up to me to decide whether I could live with that and choose the best way to help my people be their best no matter what."

It's easy to get caught up in an emotional win-lose scenario when a top decision maker believes it's time to change the rules. Instead, you can refocus your efforts to do the best for your team—even when you can't persuade the decision maker to agree with you 100 percent. I asked Elam to reflect on what she learned in her ten years as dean. During her tenure, graduate admissions had tripled, *US News & World Report* and *Business Week* consistently recognized the College of Business, and she oversaw construction of a $32 million state-of-the-art business complex for the school's seventy-five hundred students. I drew on her answers to formulate a "leadership agility" list to help shift your frame of reference the next time you run into (or anticipate) opposition.

Leadership Agility Increases Communication Intelligence

- Facts alone don't win the argument.
- There are different values and beliefs that drive people's decisions, even when there are agreements in place.
- It's easy to take a person's words at face value when he appears to support what you want to do. Be sure to confirm your interpretation of what he meant by what he said.

- Trying to understand that there are different ways of looking at the world is a *lot* more effective than getting angry.
- Avoid backing people into corners with your emotions.
- You are likely to be more successful if you can vent and then set your emotions aside, and are willing to get more information about how they see things.

To conclude the stories in Part Two, here is a memorable lesson from the world of sports, where the humility it takes to look deeper into a loss leads to the ability to go back out and win.

Lessons From a Winner When Things Went Wrong

What happens when you "lose it" and you need to "Take 10" with your inner critic?

Sometimes the most important pause of all is to stop to listen to an inner voice. Call it your gut, intuition, or a hunch; it takes time to sort it through when there's so much going on and you're under pressure to perform.

Athletes are some of the highest-performing people we have the opportunity to observe over time as they perfect their skills in front of fans and the media. One of those high-wire artists is an exuberant young pitcher, the "closer" for the Boston Red Sox. A few years ago, Jonathan Papelbon *wasn't* known for keeping his cool when things got hot in the game. However, three years of being in the pressure cooker of a top-rated team and winning baseball's coveted World Series championship have taught him the power of self-reflection. That's what he needed to turn to one night, after an adrenaline-charged loss.

This was the second loss in a row for Papelbon; he was stunned as he walked off the mound having "blown" a ninth-inning lead. I heard the television announcers saying that something must be wrong because Papelbon was sitting on the bench in the dugout by himself, just staring down with his face buried in his hands.[1] And he did sit there — for ten minutes — in front of the cameras, the fans, and his teammates. This wasn't the behavior they'd come to expect from the normally vocal "Pap."

"I just didn't want to get up and say something I shouldn't be saying," Papelbon explained later when he stepped up to the media microphones. "I just wanted to collect my thoughts and just think about what happened out there tonight and how I'm going to go about changing things."[2]

Later he would tell the sportswriters what he figured out as he sat there pondering what he was doing wrong. He admitted that he needed to make some adjustments in "finishing" his pitches better as they crossed the plate so that batters wouldn't be able to hit them the way they had recently been doing.

Pap had paused, in front of the cameras and thousands of fans. He had gotten a grip on himself, and in the days to follow, he regained his ability to finish his ninety-five-mile-an-hour pitches.

Whether you are in the public spotlight when things go wrong or just need to shine a light on what's not working for you, pause before you go back out into the fray. **Look inward and reclaim your power to be your best.** It worked for Papelbon. Months after his very public personal time-out, as he prepared to pitch Game 3 of the 2008 American League Championship Series playoffs, Pap had not allowed a run in his first twenty-two career postseason innings.

∞

Tips and *Yeah, Buts*

Rephrasing is the art of offering someone the gift of your valuable time and scarce attention. In your own words, you help people hear what you *think* they meant by what you heard them say. When you stick your neck out to do this, you show that you care about understanding the meaning behind people's words and that you're not making assumptions. This builds trust.

TIPS FOR USING
POWER OF PAUSE PRACTICE #5:
Use Rephrasing as a Twenty-First-Century Risk Management Tool

- Rephrasing can inspire someone to tell you more or to provide invaluable clarification. He may say, "Well, OK, and another thing . . ."
- Rephrasing gives someone a chance to tell you her priorities. She might respond by saying, "Well, yes, that's right, but after hearing you play that back to me, I realize that what's *really* important is . . ."
- You are *not* trying to be right about what someone said. You are making sure that you understood what he meant. These can be two different things.

REPHRASING SOUNDS LIKE:

"It sounds like you are saying . . ."

"If I follow what you're saying, it seems that you . . ."

"Let me see if I understand what you mean. You're concerned that . . . and your priority is . . ."

"Before we continue, I'd like to summarize what I think I
heard you say so far . . . Please set me straight if I missed
something."

REPHRASING IS NOT:

Saying what you think about what the person said.

Giving someone advice or a solution.

Giving an explanation of your actions.

Parroting back to someone exactly what she said word for word.

Providing therapy. (Good listeners can often make people
feel better, so you can have a therapeutic effect; don't
try to analyze.)

Yeah, Buts . . . on Rephrasing

Although this skill is easy to learn, and appears to be nothing
more than reformulating someone's words, there's more to
it than that. With practice you can develop the art of naturally offering your interpretation of what you think someone
meant and become adept at responding to a correction or
added information.

• • •

Yeah, but #1: **Rephrasing takes too long.**
Reality: How we invest the time we have is always a choice.

- It's not necessarily that we don't have the time to rephrase, it's that we assume it's not necessary or worth a few minutes to explore the meaning behind someone's actions or words, a look or a tone of voice. The time it takes to clear up a misunderstanding later on can cost *far* more than a few minutes spent rephrasing up front.

- Rephrasing can build trust in record time. Why? Because rephrasing shows that by checking your interpretation of what you think someone meant, you are willing to risk being corrected in the interest of mutual understanding and a more effective solution.

- Your pause to rephrase can also give the other person a chance to be more receptive to *you*. (Research into the principle of reciprocity has repeatedly confirmed this cause-and-effect relationship.)[1] This is important if either of you is stressed, if there's a conflict, or if this is a new relationship.

- In a high-tech world where personal attention is increasingly valued, people may value you more because you are taking time to check your understanding of them. You are also giving them a chance to crystallize their priorities or to provide additional data.

Yeah, but #2: Rephrasing will offend people; it sounds as if you are putting words in their mouth.
Reality: You're right; it *can* offend people, especially if you offer your interpretation with a judgmental attitude or tone.

- People usually are not offended if you pause to take a breath or two before you respond. This gives them a clue that you are genuinely trying to understand their view rather than trying to cleverly score a winning point or to persuade them that you are right. Then when you rephrase, your intention is grounded in appreciating that there is room for misinterpretation—it's normal.

- If someone takes offense at your interpretation, don't get into an argument over what he did or didn't say. Once you have cleared up the misunderstanding, try saying, "Thank you. I'm glad we're now on the same page."

Yeah, but #3: **What if I'm wrong? Won't I look stupid or make people frustrated?**
Reality: There are ways to manage that or prevent it from happening.

- Recall that we're likely to filter as much as 80 percent of what is both said and meant. So yes, at times you *will* be wrong, and it may aggravate people.
- Be aware of your pacing and tone. You don't want to sound as if you are pushing or that you are using a technique. You *do* want your energy to convey that you are willing to risk being wrong (or enlightened) in order to make sure that eventually everyone will share a common understanding.

Yeah, but #4: **Aren't there times when I should not rephrase?**
Reality: Yes, there are times when rephrasing isn't appropriate, especially if someone needs to vent, has just heard bad news, or feels ambushed. Sometimes it's better to listen.

- You might venture, "It sounds like it might help if I just listened—you're not looking for anything else from me now . . . is that about right?" She'll either agree or let you know if there is something else she wants from you.

- Don't rephrase what someone said if you are in a group and your interpretation of what he meant would be embarrassing or make it appear that you are trying to argue your point of view. Clarify your perception privately; make sure your intent is to truly understand the other person rather than to score a point.

- Never say, "You said . . ." or "I heard you say . . ." This can sound like you are right and the other person is wrong. When you say it that way, people think you are judging, reacting, or trying to be right. Even if you are sure that what you heard is what they said, let them correct you or clarify.

Yeah, Buts . . . on Getting Curious

When you want to effectively convey curiosity as a form of open-mindedness, two of the most common resistance points have to do with struggling with self-control and sincerity.

• • •

Yeah, but #1: **I'm not remotely curious; I'm furious!**
Reality: Your anger is an honest indication that you need to pause for yourself.

- Sometimes simply admitting *to yourself* that you're not curious at all, but may later regret being furious, is enough of a pause to consider the consequences of what you might be about to do in the midst of feeling embarrassed, blindsided, misunderstood, lied to, or publicly criticized. Then you can (1) constructively vent, (2) regroup, (3) consider what you don't know you don't know, (4) decide on an initial course of action, and (5) revisit the problem without anger driving your choices.

Yeah, but #2: **I'm afraid that people won't believe me when I say I'm curious.**
Reality: Don't say, "I'm curious . . ." if you aren't.

- People will tune in to the tone of your voice or the tenor of your written words. Before you speak or write, think for a moment about whether there are any cues that signal how open the other person seems to be to more discussion. (Revisit the Curiosity Cues Checklist in Chapter Six.) You could say something like, "I'd like to know more about your idea; can we explore it now, or at another time?"
- People can pick up on the energy of your thoughts or your body language even when you don't say a thing. (You've probably experienced this.) That's why it's important to be careful about what you are thinking. Even if you *don't* say what you are thinking—for example, that their idea is absurd or a waste of time—people can feel that your actions don't reflect what they sense about your demeanor.
- One last caution: it's not always the best policy to actually use the words, "I'm curious." Some people may think that you are being nosy, condescending, or sarcastic. You can avoid that trap if you use such phrases as "I'm wondering" or "Could you tell me a bit more about how that idea would work? It would help me be sure that I understand your idea."

What's Next: Ways to Work Smarter Together, Not Harder

We have already learned how the Power of Pause methodology:

1. Interrupts automatic reactions
2. Mobilizes curiosity
3. Drives better problem solving

Next we'll examine how Power of Pause practices generate smarter decisions—*especially* at times when you are dealing with groups or with change, uncertainty, or extraordinary opportunities. Those are the times that can easily trigger the impulse to react—without knowing what you don't know you don't know. As we turn the corner into Part Three, consider this reflection from Jill Bolte Taylor, Harvard brain scientist and author. During her eight-year recovery from a stroke, she gained insight into the brain's capacity to choose whether to pause or to push.

> When you're really paying attention to the richness of the present moment, that's right-minded awareness. The left hemisphere is preoccupied with the past and future, projecting fears, contemplating ideas that aren't relevant to the here and now. Once you realize you have these two different brains, you can learn to choose, moment by moment, how you want to live. Of course, you do need the push as well as the pause to function properly.[2]

PART THREE

WHAT DON'T I KNOW I DON'T KNOW?

ASK BETTER QUESTIONS TO DRIVE SUCCESS

CHAPTER 9

HOW CAN WE ENSURE SUCCESS IN TIMES OF UNCERTAINTY?

We live and work in chaotic and disruptive times. These are times that require new skills and a deeper appreciation for what it takes to lead and to make effective decisions when there is unpredictable, high-speed change.

Not that long ago, the term *disruptive* conjured a negative image. Today, owing to the high-tech revolution, the word has a new, positive connotation. It refers to the breakthroughs that unexpectedly emerge when a game-changing innovation in using technology challenges competitors and traditional business methods. Clayton Christensen of Harvard Business School advanced the concept of disruptive technology in *The Innovator's Dilemma* and later redefined it as "disruptive innovation" in *The Innovator's Solution*. He alerted companies to the importance of adapting technology to meet the future needs of customers by providing lower-priced solutions that evolve to displace established competitors. Examples of disruptive technologies are personal computers, e-books, digital photography, mobile tele-phony, cloud computing, and the Internet—none of which were recognized as disruptive when they first appeared on the market.

New technologies disrupt the workplace and also shake up how people identify with their work. The necessity of responding to these disruptions is just one reason why the nature of leadership is changing. Until recently, leaders were expected to know the answers and for the most part were also expected to tell people what to do. Today, **leadership means being able to lead in the midst of uncertainty, regardless of whether you have an immediately definitive answer. It also means being able to inspire others to take the lead—regardless of their role or rank in an organization.**

The job of a leader has changed from having knowledge to generating knowledge and inspiring and sustaining the capacity of others to learn. Leaders must demonstrate that they are open to finding answers by publicly asking the right questions. This is the reality we face when we have to choose between sticking with what we know and going beyond our comfort zone. Leaders must have the skills to acknowledge to their employees, and to their customers, what they don't know that they don't know—in such an authentic way that it inspires people to work cooperatively to chart new territories.

The more we *think* we know, the less we truly know.

One successful senior manager candidly describes the dilemma of leading in changing times.

> ∾ Perhaps I am getting a bit jaded, but I tend to believe that many managers think they are smarter, savvier, and more effective than they truly are. A number of factors feed into that: good staff that make them

114

look good; they know a lot about how things work in their field; or their own management doesn't know how good or bad they really are. I am sure there are managers who thought they were absolutely brilliant as they were driving their companies full speed into a crisis.

Having said that, truly wise managers—who want to be agile and adapt to the changes being thrown at us—know that pausing is imperative, particularly in a maelstrom. People may think you are nuts taking a time out in the midst of a storm. But it is precisely that pause that allows you to sort, process, and then focus on what needs to be done right away and what can wait till later. Most important, you have to ask yourself, What are the dependencies in the situation?

One tricky responsibility managers have today is to understand dependencies—to connect the dots between a decision and its consequences, especially when the old way of doing things is being challenged. It is not enough to identify all the moving parts—you also need to understand who or what depends on each of those parts. You can more effectively prevent chaos when you have the discipline to hit the Pause button. Here's a simplified example:

Executive: We have deep budget cuts to make; I want you to outsource our Web function for half of what we pay the staff member to do it.

Manager: OK, I can do that. Let me get back to you to make sure we understand how that change would affect our customers.

It didn't take the manager long to put the picture together for his boss about the ripple effects this decision could have. He explained:

115

- The Web site content wouldn't be updated immediately anymore—something the boss had required nightly.
- Content changes would be triaged by cost and difficulty—and could take days, not hours.
- The budget would cover only maintenance, not site design upgrades—potentially making the site less useful for the customers.

These changes could have backfired—causing problems for the boss, the organization, and its customers—if the manager didn't examine the web of dependencies of this situation. He also had to have the courage to explain the consequences to his boss rather than just assume that he had no choice. As a result, the boss made a more informed decision and reset his own expectations as well as his staff's priorities.

Next we'll survey some of the research that reveals how our ability to handle change and uncertainty is affected by our biochemistry, psychology, technology, and capacity to connect to one another. We'll also see how to apply the Power of Pause principles to achieve your goals regardless of what is happening around you.

The Paradox of Knowledge and Uncertainty

Knowledge is different from all other kinds of
resources. It constantly makes itself obsolete,
with the result that today's advanced knowledge
is tomorrow's ignorance.
—PETER DRUCKER[1]

Making Decisions

Leaders can make and implement better decisions, reports Professor David Garvin, if they have a tolerance for uncertainty, constructively explore differences, don't take things personally, and step back from assumptions to "examine underlying presumptions." He also urges decision makers to engage in active listening to ensure that others feel understood and will support the decision rather than undercut it later. Demands for certainty and "arguments backed by unassailable data" interfere with the ability to generate adequate options or enable effective evaluation.[2]

Garvin's research fits with my clients' experiences. One CEO admitted that he didn't realize how frustrated his managers were about how long he was taking to make a decision to replace a powerful executive. Three of them asked to meet with him. Realizing that they weren't in agreement about what needed to be done, the CEO rephrased his sense of their concerns, telling them he was curious about what was troubling them. "Taking the time to listen in this way shows employees that their opinions matter. I also learned a valuable lesson. They didn't understand my own decision-making process. Now they know that when my decisions aren't coming as quickly as they would like, it's not that I'm unable to make the decision; I'm taking the time to look at all of the facts and make the best decision for our company. I also shared the reasons a particular decision was so difficult. The lesson for me was that I can't assume that people understand what *I'm* thinking or even saying."

As we see in the personal, real-time comments posted by leaders on their Web sites and in blogs, videos, and virtual cyberspace meetings—more decision makers are

117

acknowledging the need to build trust by making their thought process more transparent.

> *Power of Pause applied*: Rephrase to assure others that you didn't just hear what they said; you understood what they meant.

New Ways of Thinking

To succeed in the future, organizations need to cultivate resilience—an ability to balance between independent thinking and interdependence to foster collaboration among people with diverse outlooks. That is the view of Thomas Homer-Dixon, author of *The Ingenuity Gap*, who believes that most of us aren't well equipped to adapt to a world of constant change. His prescription? He urges us to "develop a prospective mind, a mind not fixed on the status quo, one that instead is comfortable with constant change, radical surprise, even a breakdown . . . and must constantly anticipate a wide variety of futures."[3]

One of the phrases my clients and audiences often hear me say is, **"I'm not here to make you comfortable with change. I'm here to help you be comfortable with your discomfort."** That's why Homer-Dixon's advice resonated with me. For example, when one client was recruited to leave his job as a university provost to become chancellor of a large and turbulent state university system, he didn't realize how much conflict was awaiting him in his new job, which required him to work closely with state legislators. Trained as a political scientist and having played a primary role in running a large and rapidly expanding urban university, he thought he was prepared for the politics. After a rough first year, he decided to get curious about what he could do differently.

He asked me to interview powerful legislative insiders to find out what he needed to do to be more effective. He wanted them to speak to me as his executive coach and as an objective observer, assuring them that I would relay their unvarnished comments. They were astonished and impressed that he was willing to initiate this personal (and humbling) inquiry into what he needed to improve. As a result, he was able to change the way he collaborated with them. Eventually he accomplished a number of major goals he had thought to be impossible.

Power of Pause applied: Being curious and exercising humility build trust that helps you lead, manage change, and inspire risk-taking innovation.

Continuous Partial Attention

Around-the-clock access to technology is changing our capacity to provide full attention to people and to tasks. Writing in *Scientific American Mind*, the directors of the UCLA Memory and Aging Research Center offer this insight about the impact of continuous partial attention on people and the choices they make: "They no longer have time to reflect, contemplate or make thoughtful decisions. Instead they exist in a sense of constant crisis—on alert for a new contact or bit of exciting news or information at any moment. Once people get used to this state, they tend to thrive on the perpetual connectivity."[4]

Organizations are experimenting with ways to balance the benefits of instant information devices with the need for undivided attention and respect. In one case, after sales meetings had become a battle for attention, the senior manager had the presence of mind to experiment. He decided to collect everyone's communication devices at the start of the meeting and return them at the end. As a result, sales and lead generation improved. Customer service also improved, because they made sure that other team members were better prepared to take care of the customer in their absence.

Power of Pause applied: Temporarily designating a specific amount of time to disconnect from constant information streams gives you and others a chance to focus and get more done.

Our Effect on Others

Neuroscientists keep enlightening us about how the biology of emotions drives the brain's reactions. Italian scientists recently discovered the phenomenon of mirror neurons that help us attune ourselves to the actions of others, which is what happens, for example, when you feel that you and another person on are the same "wavelength." Some neuroscientists claim to have identified mirror systems for emotion and have argued that activation of these systems may be a basis for empathy. Experts have identified empathy—the ability to read and interpret emotional cues—as one of the most important skills that enable business leaders to make *intelligent* decisions.

Other research shows that if you put someone in a meeting who has a positive outlook, that emotion can be contagious. **This research has implications for when you are trying to engage people in collaboration.** For example, data revealed that top-performing leaders foster an environment where laughter—the shared experience of not taking things too seriously at times—is more prevalent than in groups managed by midperforming leaders.[5]

Power of Pause applied: Pausing to tune in to what's going on for you and for others increases the chance for greater cooperation.

• • •

As you will see in the upcoming story, a sense of humor is invaluable, especially when helping your team or colleagues manage the stress of shifting priorities and heavy workloads. For years I've taught that it's important to laugh at oneself and to laugh with (not at) others when we discover a counterproductive habit. As the research confirms, a little levity lowers what I call "de-fences." When we're able to see the humor in a situation, we're less likely to put up the fences to keep people or ideas at arm's length and less likely to take things personally. When we aren't putting up barriers, we can move ahead with less effort.

POWER OF PAUSE PRACTICE #7:
Ask: What's on Your Plate?

Responding to competition, time pressure, new technology, or budget cuts can leave you and your staff with too much on your plates. That's what information technology resource executive Ramon Padilla and his colleagues faced as they tried their best to cope with increasingly "impossible" workloads and layoffs.

Ramon's boss, Chancellor Mark Rosenberg, asked me to develop a Work Smarter Together, Not Harder program for the government agency that supports eleven state universities, approximately three hundred thousand students, and seventy-six thousand faculty and staff. In the aftermath of significant staff cutbacks, managers were concerned about managing conflicting priorities. I told them a brief story about a practice I'd developed early in my management career.

∞ I was a twenty-something manager at the Westinghouse Broadcasting station in Boston and had been promoted to create and run a department of eight, never having directly managed more than an intern. One day after the weekly staff meeting, my talented senior publicist looked overwhelmed. I privately asked her if I could help. She hesitated, not wanting to complain, as she was proud of getting her work done. "My problem," she blurted, "is that my to-do list keeps getting longer and longer with all that you keep adding to it."

I told her we could review her priorities. "That's just the problem," she explained. "It seems that everything you give us is a top priority, and to our internal customers everything is a top priority too."

Of course she thought everything was a priority; she had no way of knowing that what had been important on Monday was less important by Wednesday because of a decision made at corporate about something happening next week. It had also never occurred to me that her plate was full, because she hadn't complained. Trying to keep things simple, I came up with the idea of a quick weekly "plate check" where we could add, drop, and shuffle projects and deadlines depending on current realities. The goal, however, *wasn't* to have me always reset the priorities; it was to develop her ability to prioritize and to handle the changes herself.

Today, the greater challenge I see for organizations is this: **few people feel that they have a *choice* or the authority to prioritize, to redistribute, or to take work off their plates.** They don't want to look overburdened or incapable and don't want to complain to their bosses, even if they complain privately, producing a chorus of discord in the workplace. So they continue to work with too much on their plates. And there are consequences because it is not a sustainable state—people can't be or do their best. That's why I challenge clients to routinely pare down and reorder their priorities with staff, which is what Ramon did shortly after the Work Smarter Together, Not Harder program.

How Are We Supposed to Prioritize in a Nonstop Workplace?

How to prevent staff burnout and achieve extraordinary performance

Two years later, Ramon had been promoted to assistant vice chancellor for information resource management. He shared how he had adapted and implemented Power of Pause Practice #7: *Ask*: What's on Your Plate?

Your personal story about being a manager made me realize that I had assumed my open-door policy created a safe environment where staff could discuss their workload with me. I also assumed that if no one was complaining, I could add more to their plate. You opened my eyes to see that most employees will not voluntarily step up to say that you (the boss) are "piling it on." I began to do regular plate checks with my employees to make sure that I wasn't burning them out.

Using the "How full is your plate?" question — as a device to open the door to efficiently communicating one's workload — has been extremely successful. The staff is poking their heads in my door to say, "Boss, there is no more room on my plate unless you have someone help me eat these mashed potatoes." This makes it easier to have a short conversation about prioritization or passing some work to someone else. "Plate check" has become part of our vernacular. However, as I write this I realize that my plate has gotten to be overwhelming, and our plate checks aren't as regular as I would like them to be.

As the manager of a shrinking IT department, Ramon has found that the plate check helps his staff keep their sense of humor. Everyone knows that the weekly staff meeting begins with these questions:

1. What's on your plate?
2. Tell me about it: What state is it in?
3. What's keeping you from clearing it?

His team takes the plate analogy and runs with it, asking questions that make it easy for them to laugh, focus, and be more effective: *What will it take to get it off your plate? Does it taste bad? Do you need a different utensil?* Ramon explains:

> *Someone might say to me, "If I have to eat this one more time, I will throw up." I'll say to them, "OK what can I do to make it taste better?" They'll shoot right back with an answer such as, "Can you get the universities (our customers) to submit their data in this type of format? It would make it so much easier." Suddenly I have a practical way to help my people get their jobs done. My approach is to build up this person's belief in themselves so that they can hold their head up and handle what's on their plate.*

By the time Ramon's staff meeting is finished, his people are managing their workloads and helping one another with little redirection from him. Using this practice has an exponential effect by increasing the effectiveness of an entire group. Ramon points out that plate checks provided other unexpected bonuses. "We became more effective because we could be more flexible and juggle our assignments when things changed without warning. With budget cuts these days, it's not like I can hand out bonuses, or give my staff a $100 gift certificate when I 'catch them doing something right.' What I can offer them is an environment where people really want to come to work. This upbeat approach is one of those little things that do just that."

CHAPTER 10

DRIVE SUCCESS WITH AN EXTRA MEASURE OF HUMILITY

When we hear the word "humility," many people think it only means, *OK, I'm going to be humble and give other people credit for a job well done.* However, there's more to humility that just modesty. In *Good to Great*, author Jim Collins researched traits of what he calls Level 5 executives—those at the top of the leadership pyramid whose companies sustain success over the long term. They "build enduring greatness through a paradoxical blend of personal humility and professional will. . . . It's not that Level 5 leaders have no ego or ambition. Indeed, they are incredibly ambitious—but their ambition is first and foremost for the institution, not for themselves."[1]

POWER OF PAUSE PRACTICE #8:
Ask: What Don't I Know I Don't Know?

Let me propose an additional dimension to the concept of humility that goes a step beyond being modest, sharing credit, or nurturing successors. **We need a new success model that acknowledges there is power in admitting that you don't know what you don't know.** What's current today is old tomorrow. This reality makes it all the more important that we be humble enough to ask ourselves, *What don't I know I don't know?* and make that attitude a twenty-first-century sign of leadership.

Experience is no longer enough of a foundation for decision making. Up until now in this book, we've been talking about the power you gain in a single pause that—like the clutch on a car—has enabled you to suspend the action for a moment to assess the situation. As you saw in Figures I.1 and 2.1, a pause is an important intervention, a way to interrupt your normal routine.

When you go several steps beyond the initial pause, after you have shifted from being furious to curious—or shifted from speeding into action to suspended animation—you arrive at the beginning of Pause 2.0, in which something more than enlightened strategy or problem solving is taking place. You give yourself the chance to personally transform how you respond, not just by focusing on the moment or the problem, but by asking yourself, *What will I do differently from now on—given what I now know that I didn't know?* (See Figure 10.1.)

Figure 10.1. Pause 2.0: Synchronize for Success

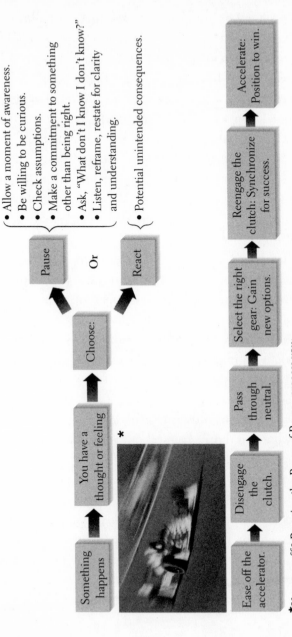

Something happens → You have a thought or feeling* → Choose: → Pause **Or** React

Pause:
- Allow a moment of awareness.
- Be willing to be curious.
- Check assumptions.
- Make a commitment to something other than being right.
- Ask, "What don't I know I don't know?"
- Listen, reframe, restate for clarity and understanding.

React:
- Potential unintended consequences.

Ease off the accelerator. → Disengage the clutch. → Pass through neutral. → Select the right gear: Gain new options. → Reengage the clutch: Synchronize for success. → Accelerate: Position to win.

*Your payoff? By using the *Power of Pause* process you:
- Retake control.
- Maximize options.
- Minimize effort.
- Apply personal power where it's needed most.
- Make a conscious commitment to change.

A moment of humility acts like a prism: it allows you to see new facets of yourself and others that you couldn't see before. **The reality hasn't changed, but your vision of it and yourself has changed, and that is the Pause 2.0 moment.** As you read in Chapter Eight, that's what happened for Dean Elam when she made the choice to see past her interpretation of the facts. After feeling blindsided by her boss's decision to revoke the bonuses her marketing staff had earned, she changed her focus. She stepped outside her reality to ask herself, *OK, what would it be like for him to give out bonuses to my staff when he's laying off faculty?*

The dean's insight came when she realized that she used to see her boss (any boss) as the enemy; now she sees him as "someone who is struggling against many odds trying to do the best job that he can." Today she is more interested in understanding how others see things than in rallying people to take her side in a dispute. This puts her in a more powerful position—to lead from her strengths.

Sometimes the most powerful decision you make is to accept what you didn't know about yourself.

As you will see in the next story, humility becomes transformational when you:

1. Suspend your perspective, however hard earned it may be
2. Admit you don't have all the answers
3. Assume responsibility to create new solutions with the candid input of others
4. Make a conscious commitment to change

Remember the Effectiveness Equation: first there is the pause, then there is curiosity, then a shift in awareness that fuels humility and yields a perspective you would otherwise not see:

Pause (Presence of Mind) + Curiosity + Humility = Professional Effectiveness and Personal Fulfillment

When Rapid Growth Creates Bottlenecks

The consequences of rapid growth and business mergers can be profitable and also humbling—especially when you find yourself dealing with situations you've never encountered or didn't expect. Integrating systems and teaming up with new strategic partners may mean that your people can't keep pace with the rate of change demanded by your customers and regulators or by your own vision. You may receive or provide training in how to handle the new rules or technology. However, there's often little training and even less attention paid to giving managers and employees the authority to make decisions they've never made before.

This next case history shows what happened when, about a year after a large merger, two executives sat in on what promised to be a contentious senior managers' meeting and discovered that their staff's rancor was just a part of the larger problem. What they learned about their blind spots surprised them and helped them see that they needed to listen with an open mind and give more authority to the next generation of decision makers.

THE POWER OF PAUSE

Why Didn't We Know How to Get to the Bottom of This Sooner?

How do you remove the blinders that keep you from seeing the real problem *and* from uncovering the unexpected solutions?

Think about the last time you finally got to the bottom of a problem and later found yourself wondering what took you so long to see what you couldn't see.

That's the issue that Tony Caron (COO) and Steve Hayworth (CEO) of Gibraltar Private Bank & Trust Company along with senior managers and their staff faced at their very successful bank. Gibraltar was one of my clients; in eighteen months it had grown from four branches to seven and expanded from approximately 100 to 240 employees. In the past, complaints from employees had been routine and manageable. After the merger, however, complaints had multiplied in size and scope. Profits were also declining at the same time as industry margins were under pressure. One day I asked a senior manager, "Look, what's the overriding problem here? Where do we start?" He shot back at me, "There are just too damn many bottlenecks in authority and decision making!"

Admitting that they were puzzled about why these persistent problems hadn't been solved, Hayworth and Caron approved my recommendation that we organize a first-ever "Bottleneck Meeting." One staff member commented, "It will be the old battle between sales and operations." Another declared, "Everyone is coming into that room thinking there is going to be a winner or a loser." In fact, however, when they left they weren't pointing fingers at each other anymore, and problems were being solved in days and weeks, not months and years.

Looking back two years later, Caron and Hayworth reflected on what they had learned about running a rapidly growing company and about what their employees needed from them in order to do their best work. Their insights are outlined in steps that you can adapt to your own situation. Steps 1 through 9 are shared by COO Tony Caron. Step 10 is CEO and founder Steve Hayworth's story.

Step 1: Invest in an Enforced Pause

Normally in our industry, it's unusual to get managers and their top reports together from across the company all in one room, other than for an annual meeting to bring everyone up to speed on strategy. The work and problem solving is handled in departments. The Bottleneck Meeting became an enforced pause to make us step back and see what we weren't seeing.

Step 2: Prepare for the Bottleneck Meeting

You advised us to ask the department heads and key senior managers to first meet openly with their teams in order to get specific, unfiltered input from them about their problems. Taking the input down to that level was what was most innovative about this process. You gave us a candid, time-saving process that enabled them to generate a specific, detailed list of concerns and ideas. We began by using your straightforward format for effective problem resolution: "I have a complaint, I have a request, I have a beginning idea of how to solve it."

Setting in place a complaint-request-idea process was significant because it gave people permission to safely state something negative without looking like a "whiner."

Step 3: Demonstrate a New Mindset

There was a debate about whether people would even feel comfortable "complaining" in front of the other departments and with the CEO sitting in. As Caron candidly admitted,

> *In the past we would have thought that the problem couldn't*
> *be that bad—because we hadn't heard complaints from*
> *clients—so it must be just staff infighting and would blow*
> *over. You helped us see that we needed to hear past the*
> *grumbling to hear what the complaints had in common.*

Step 4: Lead by Example—Rephrase

When the meeting began, I asked Caron and Hayworth to peri-odically rephrase what they thought they heard someone say and what they thought the person meant. As Caron admitted,

> *Quite a few times we had to go back and forth to really*
> *understand, not only the challenge but also, more impor-*
> *tantly, the underlying problem that hadn't surfaced yet.*
> *Convincing us to use this approach, even when it felt a bit*
> *forced at first, definitely helped us avoid being defensive. In*
> *the past we would have given excuses such as, "Well, that's*
> *just what's done in the industry" or "It's a regulation; sorry,*
> *nothing we can do about it."*

Step 5: Set Expectations

> *Even though it was awkward at first, people got past focusing*
> *on what was wrong. We invited them to challenge policies,*
> *turf, and limits of authority. We set expectations that we*
> *would focus first on issues that we could resolve quickly. We*
> *did not overpromise; we did admit that there would be higher-*
> *priority problems that would take more time to resolve.*

Step 6: Get Results by Asking, "What Don't We Know We Don't Know?"

> *We got an incredibly valuable list of approximately thirty*
> *items that weren't just complaints. We uncovered entirely new*
> *information and solutions we never would have discovered.*
> *Here's an example of a process problem that we were able to*
> *quickly resolve that signaled a new way of thinking and of*
> *problem solving.*

We had been requiring long-time clients who wanted to open an additional account, such as someone who had a checking account wanting to open a certificate of deposit, to provide us with a current driver's license (not expired). Even though they had given us a valid license years ago, in some cases the license on file had expired. Because clients are often traveling or too busy to get us an updated license, our salespeople would submit the new account forms and leave out the proof of valid (current) license. When our department in charge of approving these requests got the forms with the license information missing, they would send the forms back unapproved. The salespeople, under pressure to serve our customers and to compete with other lenders, were furious.

Our compliance department manager told us, "Look, we're required to provide a valid license as part of the new Bank Secrecy Act passed after September 11, to make sure that bank funds aren't involved in a money laundering scheme. Don't blame me; it's the law." Still, our salespeople and our clients didn't think this requirement made sense.

At the Bottleneck Meeting, our CEO paused and got curious. He'd heard about the license problem from our salespeople but never from a client. It hadn't registered as that big of a deal because we hadn't lost a customer as far as we knew. However, at this meeting we realized how much time was being wasted between departments, trading blame over whose fault it was that client requests weren't being processed fast enough.

Hayworth rephrased a bit to learn whether anyone had called the regulators to find out if there were exceptions to the rule and whether we understood the rule correctly. In a flash, I realized he was right. In the past we'd been a small bank and shared the work; we didn't have silos or specialists. I would have picked up the phone to call the regulator and had a conversation. That's exactly what I did the day after the Bottleneck Meeting. I learned that we could open a new account for an existing customer as long as we had a current license on file at the time the original account had been opened.

People had been wasting time arguing for months because they didn't know that they didn't know what someone else had assumed!

Step 7: Rethink the Way Work Gets Done

I used to see us as several groups of specialists. After the Bottleneck Meeting, I changed the way I got staff together across departments and started focusing on the bigger picture involving finance, sales, deposits, compliance, and information technology. I realized that the more we think of ourselves and others as specialists, the further away we get from knowing what we don't know.

Step 8: Resolve Decision-Making Bottlenecks

Our strict limits on how a loan was approved were another frustration for senior salespeople. We'd started the bank nearly twelve years ago as entrepreneurs and knew that once a wire transfer was made or a loan approved and funded that it was money out of the bank, so it had better be the right decision. In a high-tech world, clients expect everything to be done faster. We're also under increased pressure to react because competitors can respond more quickly, too.

*While we didn't think we had actually lost an existing customer because of our lending authority limits, in the Bottleneck Meeting our CEO was able to hear the problem differently. He could see how a senior banker would be meeting with a client out of the office and have to waste time tracking down the CEO or chief lending officer for any loan over $50,000. **In a flash it was obvious to him*** that if our people were ever to be trusted to grow and to help us grow the bank, it was time to expand their authority and get rid of a decision-making bottleneck. *With appropriate credit training for our senior people and the approval of our board, we quickly expanded their authority and offered counsel on making the right judgment calls.*

Step 9: Determine Return on Your Investment of Time

Even more important to us than the increased process efficiency was that after the meeting, we got unsolicited positive feedback from line employees. They told us that they had worked for other top companies and never been asked to provide this kind of candid input directly to their bosses—in front of other team members—and have their bosses provide it to the CEO and to the board and get fast decisions made on their suggestions.

Step 10: Resolve Communication Bottlenecks at the Top

CEO and founder Steve Hayworth identified the importance of adopting a curiosity mindset:

That first Bottleneck Meeting and the process we learned from you helped me become curious about why people feel and act the way they do. Now when I meet one-on-one or in a group, I say, I'm curious about . . . Then I'll be specific about what I'm wondering, resist the temptation to speak, and instead just listen. I've learned more about what they think and why they think it by virtue of that straightforward process. This approach lets them see that I genuinely want to understand the issue and their perspective. It also gives me the opportunity to suggest a collaborative conversation they can lead with colleagues from other areas of the company to resolve smaller matters without management intervention.

I commented that it sounded as if he was listening to understand their concerns rather than trying to persuade them to agree with him.

Hayworth replied,

> *Yes, I do listen without that agenda because I don't know what I don't know all the time. They are the ones who are with the clients in this changing environment where we don't know right now what we will be facing in the future. There's a lot of wisdom in our company that doesn't reside at the executive level.*

One result of applying the Power of Pause practices has been that regardless of what role they play, the individuals who work for Gibraltar are known as "resources for wealth and well-being"—serving time-pressed customers in ways that matter most and that also increase revenues.

∞

Putting Ideas to Work

- How could you deal effectively with bottlenecks? For example, Gibraltar designated a staff member to identify, track, and troubleshoot problems—especially when one department felt its problems were caused by another department. The company also expanded managers' decision-making authority and trained them in advanced risk analysis.
- What would it take for you to organize a Bottleneck Meeting? You could begin with the straightforward "complaint, request, potential solution" meetings in each department.

- How will you manage problem-solving expectations and priorities? Discuss and determine your decision-making criteria and be realistic: avoid overpromising.

Are We *Really* Part of a Team, or Are We a Group of Talented Individuals? (And What's the Difference?)

When working in organizations, I find that most groups of employees once called departments or divisions are now called teams. The problem is that most of the time they aren't really operating as a team. What they are is a collection of talented individuals working together in the same organization. Their bosses call them a team. They urge them to *be* a team. They give them team-building training and exercises in which the goal is for each person to coordinate his or her role with the others. Yet for a variety of commonsense reasons, it's not unusual for people to feel that they aren't really part of a team. Instead:

- Managers will call "team meetings," and the team members tolerate them, but some people don't speak candidly because it doesn't feel safe to voice their ideas, or they don't feel heard, understood, or appreciated.
- It's hard for "team spirit" to arise and survive in the soil of a leaner, high-performance, high-speed, attention- and time-constrained workday.
- There isn't a clear agreement on a set of team criteria for effective communication, problem solving, team building, equitable workload, or access to the boss.

139

In today's virtual, mobile, loyalty-challenged, cross-functional workplace of change and uncertainty, it can be harder for people to truly feel a sustained sense of teamwork. The difficulty we human beings have in forming and sustaining teams has made Patrick Lencioni's *Five Dysfunctions of a Team* a practical resource for many managers. His book allows people to understand why an unwillingness to be vulnerable and open with one another leads to a lack of trust that results in turf battles and poor communication:

The Power of Pause practices give you ways to build trust. You will be more effective when you:

1. **Pause to calm the urge to react either defensively or offensively.**

For example, taking an "enforced pause" to constructively address staff complaints or requests demonstrates a leader's commitment to being open to the need for change. Managers can collaborate with their teams to innovate and to resolve problems rather than let them fester and erode people's willingness to work together.

2. **Use the Get Curious Not Furious process and give someone the benefit of the doubt, especially when you (or your group or team) are feeling defensive.**

In one instance, departments across an organization were furious with the IT department. New software wasn't working the way they expected. The IT department insisted that it worked just fine. It was a standoff. That's when the IT department shifted gears. They got curious and agreed to observe their customers using the software at their department's workstations instead of in the IT classroom. They rephrased their customers' complaints and discovered that the customers were right: the software needed to be adapted to meet each department's needs and to meet their previously *unexpressed expectations.*

As a result, a new cross-functional problem-solving team was created. (Prior to turning this communication breakdown into a breakthrough, the IT team had been infuriating other departments by telling them, "You just need to practice using the new software; it works the way it is supposed to work.")

3. **Take responsibility to rephrase or reverse rephrase (as described in the next section).**

Several clients routinely use these two skills when one team has a problem with another or with an outside strategic partner. It's a way of taking a moment to step into another person's shoes to foster understanding on the spot instead of arguing over who is right or who is wrong.

POWER OF PAUSE PRACTICE #9:
Take Responsibility for Being Understood: Reverse Rephrase

There's another way that humility can drive more effective choices. One time-saving and relationship-building choice we can make is to take responsibility *up front* for being understood. It's a practice that I strongly encourage my clients to adopt. Pausing to make this choice—to confirm that you have been understood—is a sign of communication intelligence (CQ). As explained in Chapter Three, **CQ begins with cultivating a focused state of mind as an antidote to the urge to react.**

141

Let's be realistic. Few of us expect people to offer to rephrase what they think we meant. That's why I encourage you to prevent the likely possibility of being misunderstood: ask someone to help you make sure that what you said came through the way that you meant. I call this practice *reverse rephrasing*. It's a concept I began teaching after realizing I needed a way to help clients *prevent* costly, time-wasting "missed understandings" that were happening ever more frequently.

Years ago it occurred to me that rephrasing alone wasn't enough to prevent decision-making and communication breakdowns. Given the research on how our brain and attention span are challenged, it's presumptuous to assume that people can provide full attention, even on their best day. It was time to challenge leaders to proactively take "response-ability" for being understood.

It's very important for you to have the right intention when you approach applying this practice: by asking someone to rephrase what he thought you meant, you are *not* checking to see whether he was "listening." You *are* checking for his interpretation of your meaning and whether or not you even said what you were thinking inside your fast-moving brain. By adopting this intention and frame of mind when making your request for reverse rephrasing, you help ensure that you don't come across as condescending.

It takes an extra measure of humility to use this advanced CQ skill. It takes someone who is willing *not* to take it personally when she hears someone's "filtered" interpretation of what he said. Sticking your neck out to ask that someone rephrase what he thinks you meant also gives you a chance to discover whether your message has been heard and was unambiguously clear. Reverse rephrasing is especially useful when you are covering new or complex concepts, have been speaking for a while, or are giving difficult news, instructions, or performance evaluations.

As we'll see in the next story, the response to reverse rephrasing can also save you time in selling your idea. You'll have more time for closing the deal or enabling others to hear influential positive feedback or, even better, an endorsement. These are the results you gain in a short amount of time when you practice the self-discipline (the emotional intelligence) that helps increase your communication intelligence.

When You Have Only Fifteen Minutes (or Less) to Make Your Case

How much are you willing to risk to find out what a prospective customer thinks?

∞

One day, a client from the Center for Applied Special Technology (CAST) called me with exciting news: he had been asked to present a new technology at a meeting at the White House. The vice president would be attending. The government was interested in whether NASA could use the organization's sophisticated educational software technology to teach new skills to astronauts. The meeting could result in a NASA contract and put CAST on the map. Here's how the call began:

The opportunity: "We're thrilled at the chance to meet at the White House with the vice president and tell him all about our incredible technology and our mission."

The problem: "We only have fifteen minutes to speak!"

Their question for me: "How can we best communicate our message in that time?"

My answer: I paused. Then I said, "That's easy; just speak for 7.5 minutes and stop."

The reaction: Silence at the end of the line.

The second reaction: The clients didn't think they'd heard me correctly. So they repeated that they had only fifteen minutes and that this was a big problem. It wasn't nearly enough time to explain a complicated, exciting project that could expose the world to their technology.

Reverse rephrasing was the answer: I explained the concept of reverse rephrasing: less is more in an "overcommunicated" world. "After using *half* of your time, you should pause your presentation, then say, 'Mr. Vice President, we'd like to pause for a moment before we go on with more details to hear what you think you heard us say—so that we can make sure we've been clear about what we've explained so far."

What happened in Washington? They clocked their 7.5 minutes, paused, and did exactly as I'd coached them. Then they held their breath . . .

The reaction in Washington: The vice president apparently let them have it. No, it's not what you think. They reported that he was impressed with what he had heard, and told everyone not only that he understood their technology and what their technology could deliver but also that he thought it was brilliant and necessary, and that he supported it. They didn't need to add a word to their presentation. Apparently the vice president used up the rest of their sales time by extolling the virtues of CAST in front of an important audience.

∞

Putting Ideas to Work

This story shows the type of results you can get when you shift your attention from selling an idea to taking responsibility for how you were interpreted. The cofounders of CAST used reverse rephrasing for the first time in a high-stakes situation; it worked beyond their imagination. (Tips on how and when to use reverse rephrasing are in Chapter Fourteen.)

- What are some low-risk situations where you could begin practicing reverse rephrasing (for example, at a staff meeting, with a colleague, or with a longtime client)?
- How might you turn a potential misinterpretation of your communication into an opportunity to learn more about the other person's frame of reference?

Here's an ancient outlook on the power of words to get to the heart of meaning:

> Trying to understand from words is like washing
> a dirt clod in muddy water. But if you don't use
> words to gain understanding, it's like trying to fit
> a square peg into a round hole.
> —MASTER YUAN-WU KEGIN (1063–1135)

CHAPTER 11

REVISITING THE RESENTMENT BANK ACCOUNT

DEPOSITS AND WITHDRAWALS

As you've probably experienced yourself, there are times when words can feel like bullets, even though that's rarely what was intended. One reason we are caught off guard at work—by customers, patients, colleagues, vendors, bosses, or other people we deal with—is that we have set off their "trigger," or they have pulled ours. That's where the Resentment Bank Account is an important idea to remember.

Here's how collecting resentments becomes an unconscious habit and how you can keep this habit from creeping up on you. Each time someone does something that leaves you feeling frustrated or threatened, and you don't get to the bottom of the problem to resolve it, you are unconsciously putting deposits in your Resentment Bank Account. In some cases, you may decide to put up with the problem (or person) by saying to yourself, *It's just a little thing, it's not worth the hassle to deal with it.* But each time that it happens, your resentment builds up—with that person *or* with someone else who does something similar. In other cases, maybe the problem *isn't* a little thing—it's serious. However, you don't feel you can do anything about it, so you tolerate the situation or hope that it (or the person) will go away. But it doesn't.

Meanwhile, your deposits are earning interest, building up your account from the many times that you feel that you have been wronged. The more interest you collect in your Resentment Bank Account, the less interest you have in the possibility that there's something you have assumed or that you missed or that you don't know you don't know—about the person or the situation that keeps bothering you.

Resentments Trigger Reactions

Time goes by and then one day, when you least expect it, some unsuspecting person does the very thing that you have been putting up with. You're human, and you've had it! Now you are triggered. Suddenly you can't handle the balance of resentments that you've been stuffing in your account, so you lash out. You may speak out or gossip or even quit.

It's important to catch yourself before the resentments build up. Instead you can pause to ask yourself, *What's likely to trigger me in certain situations?* It's important to learn to recognize what you have little tolerance for—for example, when you feel that others dismiss, interrupt, or exclude you. This awareness about your tendency (in the past) to react in such situations helps you become less prone to being triggered when someone steps across your invisible boundary. When I was teaching a communication course at

Tufts University, I helped students arm themselves with this knowledge. They learned that knowing their triggers enabled them to disarm their tendency to react. As they put it, "We wish we'd known about triggers when we were younger!"

The exercise I gave the students is one that I often give to executives, when they wonder why they keep running into the same kinds of people or situations that block their ability to succeed. We can routinely become defensive or aggressive when someone's behavior goes against our view of the world—our expectations, our values, our self-image, and even the roles we played in our family.[1] When we unexpectedly encounter this challenge to our way of thinking, we're caught off guard, and that can trigger our automatic (self-protective) reactions. The next time that happens to you or to someone you are managing or working with, I suggest that you walk yourself or them through the "Know Your Trigger Points" exercise in the Tips and *Yeah, buts* section for Part Three. You can gain an important insight that might save you (or someone you're dealing with) from a lifetime of counterproductive, dispiriting resentment.

POWER OF PAUSE PRACTICE #10:
Make Withdrawals from the Resentment Bank Account

Let's look at an example of how becoming aware of "banked" resentments can lead to enlightened choices when you feel that you've been backed into a corner. Imagine that officials from your distant corporate headquarters decide, without consulting you, to spend money to support a local charity near your branch. They think this will satisfy your complaints that their failure to invest in meaningful goodwill outreach puts you at a disadvantage with the locally owned competition.

However, the charity isn't even in your customers' town. You resent that *once again* corporate hasn't bothered to check with you first. You're angry because you've got to give up your first weekend off in months to volunteer for the charity's park clean-up event that isn't even benefiting your customers. You feel trapped because now you are expected to be grateful that the company responded. What you'd really like to tell corporate is that they have no clue about what they are doing!

You don't know it yet, but your Resentment Bank Account is full and you're ready to unload it—at a colleague, a customer, or someone else. What can you do? Use the Effectiveness Equation shortcuts to shift your mindset and your actions:

1. **Practice the Power of Pause process.** Instead of feeling resigned or powerless, realize that you *do* have a choice about how to handle this.
2. **Use the Get Curious Not Furious approach** and start asking yourself what you may have assumed about the other person's intentions when he made a choice that didn't meet your needs.
3. **Ask yourself,** *What Don't I Know I Don't Know*—about what is triggering me or what's triggering them?

Like many people, you work in a company that's been acquired more than once, and you're dealing with new managers and policies. Again! That is another reason why you are

150

sick and tired of people making decisions for you and your team, without so much as talking to you on the phone or sending an e-mail to discuss your ideas. Take a minute to ask yourself, *Do I get triggered when I don't feel heard?*

By using the Power of Pause practices to shift your mindset, you are less invested in being right and assuming they are wrong. That alone can shift your frame of mind into neutral and clear your head. It has taken you only a few minutes to go through this three-step mental exercise of reframing your assumptions and understanding your trigger. It's giving you the choice to see "corporate" with a different view. With your resentment on hold, you can speculate more constructively about possibilities you couldn't imagine when you were feeling ignored. You think to yourself, *Maybe the people at corporate who made this decision were under the gun to spend charitable dollars before they expired from the budget. Or maybe they were trying to take initiative.*

Because you avoided reacting from resentment, you are now in a better position to lobby for what's best for your customers and employees. You can send an e-mail or pick up the phone to have a conversation. You begin by appreciating your colleagues' effort to respond to your request for community outreach. Then, taking responsibility for what you don't know you don't know, you realize that it may not be their fault that they didn't pick the right project. You appreciate that they made a good-faith effort. So, you give them an update, letting them know about a popular local charity that you'd like to put at the top of the list for goodwill outreach next time.

Considering how easy it is to be disappointed or hold a grudge, I'm not saying that it's realistic to *close* your

Resentment Bank Account. However, when you develop the habit of pausing and being curious about what you or someone else may have assumed, you'll spend less time keeping score about "missed understandings." Instead, you can profit from new opportunities you wouldn't have discovered when your bank account was full of resentments that were blocking the way.

TIPS AND *YEAH, BUTS*

TIPS FOR USING
POWER OF PAUSE PRACTICE #8:
Ask: What Don't I Know I Don't Know?

How are we supposed to interrupt our tendency to react when we're triggered or when a decision is called for right away? I'm suggesting that you use a simple phrase to help you shift from jumping to a conclusion, even if you think you are right and have the facts. Ask yourself this seven-word question: *What don't I know I don't know?* Just like the phrase Get Curious Not Furious, this single sentence has helped clients and thousands of others give themselves an extra measure of insight when they're feeling challenged.

What's it worth to you or those you manage to have at your fingertips an instant "attitude adjustment accelerator"? That's what happens when you ask yourself, *What don't I know I don't know?* Business adviser Logan Loomis explains that's exactly what happened one day during a rapidly unfolding situation with a client. "A CEO called me because he was furious about an action from his board of directors. I suggested that he pause and ask, *What don't I know that I don't know?* He then got curious, and quickly discovered that the board's action had not been communicated as intended. Later he called to thank me: "Thank God I didn't do what I initially wanted to do!"

There are times you are tempted to rush to react, especially when you feel that you are right or justified, or that you don't have the time to research what went wrong. However, when you choose to reconsider your assumptions you give yourself a chance to quickly surface insights and choose more constructive ways to respond. You can also ask yourself:

- What might I be missing?
- What don't I know is driving the other person or driving me?
- What doesn't she know that she doesn't know about the situation or me or even herself?
- How might we be in the same boat and not even know it?
- Can I just appreciate where he is coming from without needing to agree with him?

TIPS FOR USING
POWER OF PAUSE PRACTICE #9:
Take Responsibility for Being Understood: Use Reverse Rephrasing

Reverse rephrasing enhances your ability to nip misunderstanding in the bud, especially when you are dealing with complexity, deadlines, or a difference of opinion. It is a way to take responsibility for being understood *before* something goes wrong.

ADOPT THE RIGHT MINDSET

- This is a proactive, snafu-preventing leadership skill, and it takes time to master.
- Be patient with yourself; it's good to practice at first in low-risk situations.

- Before you take this course of action, it's important to make sure that you have *your* expectations in check: you *aren't* expecting to be completely understood.

DEMONSTRATE COMMUNICATION INTELLIGENCE

Realize that you may have:
- Left important information out of your communication
- Thought you said something that you meant to say, but didn't
- Been unaware of how your tone, pace, attitude, facial expressions, or timing may have caused your meaning to be misconstrued—even if you thought that your words *or* intentions were perfectly clear

REVERSE REPHRASING SOUNDS LIKE:

"I'd appreciate it if you would do me a favor. We've covered a lot of ground, and I want to make sure that I've been clear and haven't missed something important. Could you just run by me a few key points that stuck with you about what I said in case I wasn't clear or left something out?"

WHAT REVERSE REPHRASING IS NOT

- When you ask someone to reverse rephrase, you are not asking him to repeat your words.
- Reverse rephrasing *isn't* a test of whether someone was listening; it's a way to confirm her understanding of what you meant, not what you said. It gives you a nonconfrontational way, before it's too late, to clarify the meaning behind your messages.

155

- If you sense that someone isn't listening, it's *not* appropriate to ask him to reverse rephrase. Instead, consider what might be on his plate that *you* missed. Without making assumptions, decide if this is a good time to acknowledge, "Let me stop before we go any further and get your sense of what I'm saying. I may have left something out or need to clarify." Then pause and listen.

ACTIVATE YOUR HUMILITY

- Remember, in a world of attention spans diminished by distractions and filters, most of what you say can go in one ear and out the other even when someone thinks she is paying attention.
- Don't take it personally when people forget your first or last or middle points or if you think that they weren't listening to you.

POWER OF PAUSE PRACTICE #11:
Know Your Trigger Points (and Theirs)

It doesn't take much to feel backed into a corner. That's why it makes sense to have a safety catch to protect us against rapid-response reactions. One helpful practice that can raise your communication intelligence is to know what triggers you. Being aware of your own sensitivities makes you more effective because you are able to take more control over circumstances where otherwise you would tend to overreact.

We all have patterns of reactions, and we see them play out every day. In a her article "The Answer to Anger and Aggression Is Patience," author Pema Chodron points out that the path to regaining self-control lies in having the patience to be inquisitive about our patterns of reacting to people and situations. She writes, "The path is a journey of investigation, beginning to look more deeply at what's going on. . . . Aggression, on the other hand, prevents us from looking: it puts a tight lid on our curiosity. Aggression is an energy that is determined to resolve the situation into a hard, solid, fixed pattern in which somebody wins and somebody loses."[1]

The Exercise

Think about situations in which you are likely to be triggered (for example, when you are being manipulated, pressured, dismissed, blindsided, snapped at, taken for granted, or lied to through omission). Ask yourself now, or the next time you feel that you are having a strong reaction to something someone said or did:

1. What event, words, action, type of person, or behavior set me off, triggering a rapid reaction that kept me from being or doing my best?
2. What really bothers me most is when someone . . .

Answering these two questions raises your awareness of the types of situations that trigger you, and thus increases your ability to pause. As a result, you are less likely to automatically take something personally. This knowledge gives you a chance to shift to neutral and stay in control of your reactions. (Think back to George's story in Chapters Three and Four when he rethought his response once he realized he was reacting to being triggered when he felt blindsided.)

Becoming aware of *other* people's trigger points will also give you a time- and relationship-saving advantage: you can give someone the benefit of the doubt or avoid hitting his hot button altogether. Given the law of reciprocity, over time he may do the same for you.

Yeah, Buts . . . on Reverse Rephrasing

Yeah, but #1: Asking people to reverse rephrase sounds as if I'm testing them.
Reality: Yes, it can sound like that if you don't preface your request with sincere words, tone, and body language.

- Actually, you are the one being "tested" to see how well you were able to convey your message. You are appreciating that each person's world is full of internal conversations and external distractions.
- When you ask someone to replay a few key points he thinks he heard you say, the key to being successful with this request is to be 100 percent sincere. Ways to reinforce your sincerity include:

  1. Resisting the urge to rush your request: pace yourself
  2. Setting aside expectations for what you are about to hear
  3. Pausing to appreciate the person's effort before you follow up to clarify what he offered you

Yeah, but #2: Won't I look like an ineffective leader if I sound as if I'm not sure of my own ability to communicate?
Reality: This is a very valid question, and here's how I see it. To be effective in a fast-paced, changing workplace, leaders must be willing to acknowledge that they don't have all the answers and that it's essential to check assumptions. Reverse rephrasing shows that you are committed to communication that gets the job done.

- Leaders with high CQ have the humility to appreciate that much of what anyone says can get lost in translation. Agile, resilient leaders aren't threatened by transparent communication practices. Reverse rephrasing is one step to help ensure that what you said is what someone heard and what was heard is what you meant to say. And if there's a need for you to clarify, you welcome that opportunity.
- Leaders who want to make the most effective use of their time begin by appreciating that meaning isn't in the words; it's in the interpretation of them. Reverse rephrasing is a safety check to prevent or mitigate the effects of communication being altered through the filters of cultural differences, distractions, experience, expectations, stress, and shortened attention spans.

Adopting "Response-Ability" Habits

When you adopt the habit of using the CQ tools in this book, you are taking responsibility for preventing or clarifying missed understandings. This leadership skill enables you to make sure that you and others are in sync; then you can move on to whatever needs to be done next without the costly delay of a communication snafu.

This book *also* encourages you to adopt new habits to handle change more effectively. However, making changes can be an uphill climb, and it begins not with how well you hear but with how well you listen. That's why I want to step back to offer some perspective on what it takes for an old habit, which was once acceptable, to be replaced with a new one. It starts with the pause of awareness and then shifts into a new action.

Launching the Designated Driver Program

In the United States prior to the 1980s, it was generally acceptable for people to have a few drinks and drive, as long as they weren't drunk. Although tougher drunk-driving laws had been passed, sadly they weren't enough to keep impaired drivers off the roads. In spite of widespread public service announcements, few people knew how to keep friends and family from driving after drinking too much alcohol.

In 1985, two drunk-driving teenagers caused an accident that killed a young reporter at WBZ-TV, the Boston television station where I worked. I was the editorial and communications director at the time, and my team and I persuaded management to let us launch a joint research and community action campaign with the Harvard University School of Public Health and the Massachusetts Restaurant Association. Inspired by the practice of using a designated hitter in baseball—to go to bat for someone who wasn't at the top of his game—we introduced the novel idea of designating a driver who wouldn't drink alcohol, in order to drive

REVISITING THE RESENTMENT BANK ACCOUNT

others home safely. New laws and limits were set. It became socially desirable to designate a driver.

However, it wasn't just driving drunk that was the problem! New research showed that our ability to drive safely was compromised (more than we had previously realized) before we reached that legal limit.[2] We learned that even a minor amount of impairment could cloud a driver's judgment, causing tragic mistakes. In my years of experience in working with individuals and organizations, I've found that the same is true when it comes to impaired listening: **we make poor decisions when we don't realize that we're "listening while impaired."** This happens when we are distracted or when we have figuratively "driven" past our personal limits; we are on overload and don't have the self-control (or the habit) to pause and do what it takes to prevent or manage our reactions.

Taking the On-Ramp to Change

As we learned in Part Two, at some point our filters are at work, altering the meaning of what was communicated. Simply put: we humans are wired to misunderstand. Pausing, exercising curiosity (instead of reacting), rephrasing, and reverse rephrasing are time-saving habits that enable you to be a more effective "rapid responder." This is especially important for anyone who manages or leads others or who is tasked with being the "response-able" one.

As you recall from the 3 A's process of forming a new habit (discussed in Chapter Six): **Gaining awareness is the first step toward realizing that it's time to replace an old habit with a new one.** Your decision to take a moment to reflect—to listen to your inner dialogue—is the "on-ramp" for you to access the presence of mind that sparks curiosity. Instead of dogmatically sticking to your guns, you become open to new options by exploring what you don't know that you don't know. You can see in Figure 2.1 how these steps come together as a framework for more powerful decision making.

What's Next? Producing Unimaginably Powerful Results

As you've seen in your life and in the stories you've been reading, missed understandings can provoke people to attempt to solve the wrong problem, or cause them to fail to solve the real, less obvious problem. In Part Four you will see people in a variety of professions use the Power of Pause practices to produce unimaginable results. In spite of the odds against them, they set history in motion, earn "first mover" status in the marketplace, or change the way the game is played.

These pioneers have something else in common: they take conscious risks to apply new ways of thinking—challenging others to keep learning, too. I was reminded of that lesson one morning when I came across the story of Oliver Selfridge, one of the founding fathers of artificial intelligence. I was reading the obituary pages, a habit I'd learned from my dad, who used to read them every morning before work; he taught me that it was a way to pay one's respects to people for their contributions to the world—regardless of whether you had known them. I was struck by what Oliver Selfridge

(1926–2008) had told his son when asked what motivated his quest to understand the mind:

> Learning is the real mainstream of the mind. A mind without learning is not a mind at all.[3]

PART FOUR

THE ART OF THE PAUSE

DO WHAT MATTERS MOST AND MAKE IT COUNT

CHAPTER 12

WHERE ARE WE GOING?

Where am I going? How do I get there from here? How can I do what works *and* still feel good about myself?

These are questions you may ask yourself when meeting everyday challenges, including:

- Competing to be heard—amid the distracted attention spans and stresses of employees, coworkers, family, and clients
- Launching an important project—and persuading others to trust you and implement it in ways that bring out their best and also meet your goals
- Cutting budgets—while admitting that those cuts may threaten important values
- Hiring the right people or laying off others—facing difficult choices and dealing with the consequences
- Collaborating with your colleagues, strategic partners, and competitors—weighing whether it's worth the time and effort that it takes
- Starting a new job—whether you are an associate, manager, director, or CEO

In the twenty-first century, we will continue to encounter challenges and opportunities that we cannot anticipate. We'll also grapple with unresolved, decades-old problems in the search for a breakthrough. In Part Four you'll see several pioneers and masters apply the Power of Pause principles to make history. One way that they adapt to the demands of these times is by learning the inexact art and emerging science of collaboration.

How Do We Shift to Collaborating?

Many of us face a new reality (or requirement): to succeed, we need to collaborate. This can be welcome news to some or can cause others to voice legitimate concerns, such as:

- How am I supposed to change the way I get things done when I'm used to going it alone and frankly feel that I can do it better than anyone else?
- I don't trust that others won't pirate my ideas.
- If I really say what I think about someone else's idea, I'll be branded as not being a team player.
- I'm wary of getting involved in what sounds like groupthink or endless meetings.

In workplaces around the world, managers and employees, new hires and founders are defining what collaboration means to them and how to make it work. That includes sorting through the differences between participating in brainstorming, committees, and groupthink versus engaging in a clearly articulated collaborative framework for candid, far-reaching discussion. Researchers at Georgia Tech and the University of Illinois, for example, are studying what is required to structure effective collaboration. They are evaluating better ways to manage communication, decision making, and competition. In fact, Georgia Tech's new Molecular Science and Engineering building was specifically designed to foster interdisciplinary learning by "knocking down the old traditional walls between engineering and science disciplines." Engineers now work side by side with chemists and biologists in problem-solving "neighborhoods" instead of departmental silos.[1]

While universities take steps to teach collaborative thinking and skills to the next generation, in many cases organizations aren't giving employees or managers the training or the time they need to shift their attitudes or skills to collaborate effectively *and* feel valued in the process. It takes time to learn, for example, to share information that was once closely guarded; to cooperate with one another when faced with scarce resources; to generate consensus as distinct from merely agreeing to a compromise; to apply decentralized problem solving that doesn't depend on a single leader; to provide appropriate compensation and credit for collaboratively generated results; or to operate as a virtual, electronic, international group of individuals who cocreate products on a computer screen.

Classic research studies in cooperation reveal that we appear to have inherent tendencies to work together toward a common goal, especially when certain risks or rewards are clearly understood. One of the most well known of these studies, the "prisoner's dilemma" model of cooperation and

169

conflict, emerged out of game theory in the 1950s and has stood the test of time. The basic idea of the prisoner's dilemma is that if two parties cooperate, they are both better off.

Recently this research was taken a step further when a Harvard University mathematician, Martin Nowak, a biologist in a new field called evolutionary dynamics, demonstrated in a mathematical proof that it pays to work together. He developed formulas to prove that human beings evolved to cooperate. He explains, "The most competitive scenario of natural selection, where everybody competes with everybody else, can actually lead to features like generosity and forgiveness." In studying the factors that made cooperators successful, he found that optimism mattered: "A winning strategy must be hopeful. I must assume that it will be possible to cooperate with you."[2]

One area of collaboration where new ground is being plowed is the way in which scientific research is conducted. Traditionally, top scientists called the shots and competed for the credit and grants. Now funders and some key scientists are insisting that researchers work together instead of competing—because they believe that sharing data, perspectives, and techniques is essential to accelerate the pace of breakthroughs.

New technology is clearly driving high-speed change in the way that research is done, giving us new ways to be more effective. However, this first story shows that overcoming the obstacles to progress didn't require high-tech hardware but rather the skills of knowing when to set aside technology and use intuition, humane (collaborative) management, and good judgment. As you will see, choosing to pause, get curious, and exercise humility enables you to access those skills.

What's It Going to Take to Bridge Cultural Differences, Tame Egos, and Save Lives?

How do you persuade highly talented people to shift gears from competing to collaborating?

Award-winning cancer researcher Dr. Michele Carbone used to think that leading and succeeding were based on being right and telling others how to get the job done fast. Today he tells a different story, about his race to find a cause and cure for mesothelioma, a particularly virulent form of cancer, which kills most patients in less than a year after diagnosis.

∞

When Carbone began an international cancer research project in rural Turkey in the mid-1990s, he faced multiple problems: How could he resolve clashes over differences in religion, scientific methods, and language and earn the trust of doctors, villagers, funders, governments, and colleagues? How could he mobilize their curiosity to overcome anger and egos when things don't turn out as expected?

He arrived at a time of heightened political tensions between Muslim and Christian countries and a time of shrinking cancer research budgets. It was also a time when the incidence of malignant mesothelioma (MM), a fatal tumor of the membrane surrounding the lungs and associated with asbestos exposure, was increasing in the United States. Millions of people were at risk worldwide. When Carbone heard about three rural villages in Turkey with the highest occurrence of MM in the world—a virtual epidemic—he felt that Turkey was where he had to search for clues to break

171

the genetic cancer code, find a treatment and a cure, and map out a prevention plan. His story emerged during several interviews where he didn't hesitate to be candid—about learning what it takes today to make the most difference.

What Was the First Obstacle to Collaboration?

"It was me," confesses Carbone, who grew up in an Italian family of seven generations of Carbone physicians. He went on to say:

> ∞ When I began the research in Turkey ten years ago, I was younger, enthusiastic, and had a tendency to understand—in my opinionated way—what needed to be done. Then I'd tell people how to go about doing it. I wanted things done quick and right. Later I learned that what I knew was not necessarily enough. Other people had a different way of thinking and a different culture.

The Power of Listening

> ∞ At the beginning of the project at a conference in Turkey, I gave a presentation about my theory on the genetic link to cancer. At the end of the talk, one of the village pharmacists met me at the hotel. He screamed at me, insisting that genetics had absolutely nothing to do with the epidemic in his village: "There's nothing wrong with our genes. You are wrong, wrong, wrong."
>
> Then I remembered that on the flight I'd been rereading one of my favorite books—Plato's writing about dialectics and the importance of asking the right questions. That gave me an idea. When the pharma-

cist stopped screaming, I waited a few minutes, then I said, "Listen, I respect you very much. I can tell that you really care about your people, so please tell me, why do you think they get cancer?" He started yelling again, "There is nothing wrong with our genes!"

The Power (and Discipline) of Curiosity

∞ I said slowly, with restraint, trying to be curious, "OK, if it's not genetics, then what is it?"

It took me two hours of listening to him before I heard him say the magic words, "It is their immune system; some are protected against cancer and some aren't."

I told him, "I agree with you, that's what I mean by genetics. You call it their immune system; I call it genetics."

It turns out that these two dedicated professionals, who were both trying to help the villagers, didn't realize that they were in "violent agreement." They held the same viewpoint; it just sounded as if they were 180 degrees apart because they were using different words that ultimately had the same meaning. Carbone had to bridge the communication gap between their two cultures and the interpretation of the words he had been using.

Finding Common Ground

∞ Once we had found a common point of agreement, the research project was accepted in the village because they understood now that we weren't saying that their family genes were defective. If I had insisted on using my terminology, I probably wouldn't have

173

been allowed to set foot in those villages. I learned
that you have to listen carefully to hear past what
people say to understand their concerns and motivation, because they won't immediately tell you.

Getting Started in Creating the Right Team

∞ Next I had to find the right researchers to work
with in Turkey. I started with Dr. Baris, an esteemed
elder physician who had discovered the epidemic in the
villages and treated most of the patients for twenty years.
However, he disagreed with my theory that there was a
genetic problem causing the immune system weakness.
He felt the erionite stone that the villagers' homes were
made from was causing the problem. There were two
types of erionite stone; people in the houses who got
sick had homes built with one type, while the ones who
didn't get sick lived in houses made of the other type.
Because he was held in such high esteem in the medical community, without his backing I wasn't going to
get the tissue samples I needed.

Making a Withdrawal from the Resentment
Bank Account

∞ For years I've been battling people who thought I
was wrong or too young. But I knew it was important
to have Dr. Baris on the team, so I didn't give up on
changing his mind. It took two years of collecting the
data before he was willing to take a second look. I was
stunned when he acknowledged that I was right.
It impressed me that he was willing to change his
mind instead of sticking by theories that he had

published in journals for years. At the same time, I had to be willing to change my mind, not about the science, but about how to work with people. Science cannot move forward unless you have the right people working together on your team. We've gone from disagreement and resentment to becoming close friends.

They Don't Teach You This in Medical School

∞ Dealing with local politics isn't something they teach you in medical school. When the scientists started taking blood samples and soil samples, they were verbally attacked and blocked by the villagers, who still tried to convince us that there was no "epidemic" of cancer. When they finally agreed that there was some cancer among them, they insisted it had nothing to do with their houses or their genes. Once again we were told we were wrong.

Curiosity + Humility = Trust

∞ I paused to wonder, What were the villagers thinking? So I asked them, "Why do you think you get cancer?" They screamed at me, then I quietly repeated myself, "No, you tell me—I really want to know what do you think is the problem." (By getting them involved in the discussion it shows you really care.) They asked me, "Why are you measuring the air in the street and in the houses instead of in the fields where we go to work and spend most of our time? It's because the government wants to kick us out and move us to a new village, isn't it?" I said, "OK, where do you want us to measure in the field?"

175

I knew we needed to win their trust, so we measured
the air in the field. They were right; something was
wrong with the air outside of their homes, too.

The Breakthrough

Carbone explained to me that when the erionite stone used to
build most of the houses in the villages was dug up from deep
within the earth, there was a chemical reaction. Erionite has
fibrous qualities similar to asbestos, a known carcinogen. His
theory was that this environmentally caused chemical reaction triggered cancer cells to grow in some families and not
in others. As a result of listening and stepping back from his
original research plan, to put himself in the villagers' shoes,
Carbone and the local scientists made a breakthrough discovery: there was a genetic-environmental link that could trigger
the cancer in some people and leave others untouched.

The research project had to take an entirely different
turn before the team could proceed to find a treatment and
a cure for a cancer that was killing entire families in these
remote villages. Teaming up with Dr. Murat Tuncer, director of the Department of Cancer Control and Ministry of
Health, Carbone persuaded the Turkish government to build
new housing for the villagers, relocate them, build a new
clinic (where the villagers could get medical care and be
tested), and build a road for them to get there.

Assembling and Managing an International Team

At the same time, Carbone had to put together an international team of scientists in numerous specialties and persuade
them to collaborate. I asked him, "How do you get people
with very different backgrounds and ways of seeing the world
to work together?" He explained his three-step approach:

Peers

∞ First, you have to try to encourage each individual to appreciate the others' work. Each person tends to see what he or she does as very important and what others do as not so important. For example, the geologists see the amount of work they put into studying the rock and value that very much. The molecular biologist feels that her molecular analysis is very important. The genetic expert feels that his part is the critical piece. Moreover, in the beginning these people don't know each other, and they don't work in the same institution or in the same country.

Egos

∞ The next challenge is to make people realize it's like a relay race: everyone runs a part of the race, and at the end, although only one crosses the finish line, he wouldn't have gotten there without each person running his part. We're trying to achieve this sense of everyone being equal in a field where we have a tendency to see ourselves as a prima donna. Once people understand, however, that no one can succeed alone without the others, you begin to get a group of individuals to start thinking about being parts of the whole.

Leadership

∞ Finally, you have to be a different kind of leader. You cannot have a hidden agenda—you cannot be perceived to favor anyone. You must be honest with everyone, even when you are wrong. It's also important for everyone to believe that they are working on more than just a grant, more than a career,

177

more than a paper. It is not like it was in the old days where success was about making the leader happy. We are doing this project because it is worthwhile, and no single person could achieve this alone no matter how good they are at what they do or have done.

∞

A Postscript About Seeding Innovation

There's more to the story behind what it takes to foster collaboration in a world that rewards competition. In 2005, when I was invited to become a member of the foundation board of the American Association for Cancer Research (AACR), I studied its briefing book on the complexities of cancer research. The AACR is the world's oldest and largest scientific organization focused on cancer research, with over thirty thousand members worldwide. One of the facts that caught my eye was that in many cases, it took thirty to forty years before research done in laboratories would be "translated" into providing prevention, a treatment, or a cure.

Being a curious problem solver and a communication specialist, I asked, "Why does it take this long?" Here is what the experts told me. First, for the most part, laboratory researchers and physician-scientists who treat the patients "don't speak the same language and have different motivations behind their work." One group is working in laboratories with pure science and theories, and the other is focused on clinical research and its impact on real-time patient care. Second, researchers don't usually share their data because they are competing for scarce funding resources, patents, and recognition, including major grants and the world's most prestigious scientific prizes, such as the Nobel Prize.

"Well, if that's the problem," I said to the AACR and to Kirk Landon, who oversees the family trust that was funding nearly $500,000 in cancer prizes, "let's change the incentive and reward scientists for collaborating. We'll provide grants to recognize them for overcoming the traditional competitive and communication barriers. This way it might take less time for the scientific breakthroughs to be translated from the lab to the bedside." At first, like many innovators, I faced reluctance from the experts who were hesitant to make such a change. Like Dr. Carbone, Kirk Landon and I had to combine persistence with patience and humility in order to successfully collaborate with AACR's experts to implement the new grant criteria.

Two years later, momentum for research collaboration was sparked by others: the National Institutes for Health (NIH) and the Bill and Melinda Gates Foundation initiated new multimillion-dollar medical research grant programs that required applicants to collaborate. The NIH grants also encouraged medical schools to teach collaboration as part of their curricula and even create work spaces that fostered information sharing. And, after carefully identifying its own criteria for evaluating excellence in research collaboration, in 2008 the AACR awarded the first Landon-AACR Innovator Award for International Collaboration in Cancer Research to Dr. Carbone and his dedicated, remarkable international team.[3] The grant came as Carbone's team began their second decade of building bridges "to foster respect and trust among scientists from very different cultures" and, as they will also tell you, to build bridges to peace. As the director of the Cancer Research Center of Hawaii and chairman of the Department of

Pathology at the John A. Burns School of Medicine, University of Hawaii, Carbone has a new mission: to transform Hawaii into an international cancer research gateway to foster collaboration.

When You Get to the Fork in the Road

> In life there are forks in the road. When you get to
> the fork, you can make the right choice—or not.
> —NORRIS BENDETSON'S ADVICE TO HIS SON,
> BOBBY

There are times when a challenge or opportunity crosses your path without warning. This next case history shows how you can be a catalyst for success by acknowledging what you don't know you don't know. It also gives you insight into how an ad hoc group of highly skilled individuals discovers ways to work together.

Investing in Our Common Humanity: One Conversation at a Time

How do you motivate people to pursue the "impossible"— to choose words over weapons?

When the stakes are high, how do you pave the way for a breakthrough? You may encounter resistance or doubt. Or, as Bobby Bendetson, CEO of the fourth-generation-owned Cabot House home furnishing chain was told, "You'd best leave it to the professionals because you're just not qualified." That didn't stop him and an unlikely cast of characters who embarked on a risky venture that unexpectedly took them on a three-year journey. Theirs is a story about the Power of

Pause, curiosity, and humility—to disarm rivals, open minds, and pioneer a path toward peace.

∞

Bobby Bendetson didn't think he'd ever have the chance to play a part in helping total strangers negotiate peace in the middle of a war. He didn't go to college to be a diplomat; he studied economics and management so that he could run the furniture company that his great-grandfather had started after he immigrated to the United States from Eastern Europe. The family felt that their education at Tufts University had helped make a difference, and they'd been generous donors over the years.

One of the projects that Bendetson, who is a Tufts trustee, and his wife, JoAnn, funded was a yearlong Politics of Fear symposium at Tufts in early 2006. The symposium was part of a Tufts program called Education for Public Inquiry and International Citizenship, at the Institute for Global Leadership, led by Sherman Teichman. His intent is to "challenge students to reassess or even jettison prior assumptions or beliefs" and to engage in global problem solving. Provost Jamshed Bharucha calls him "a force of nature who inspires transformation."

Teichman and his students convinced experts from around the world to share their stories of terror and healing at the symposium. One powerful part of the program unfolded when South Africans told their chilling accounts of how they went from being mortal enemies—dealing with torture and resistance—to finding reconciliation and peace. Panel members included:

- Hentie Botha, former Lieutenant Colonel, who served twenty-five years in the South African Police

- Aboobaker Ismail, former Commander of Special Operations, member of the Military High Command (part of the African National Congress)
- Mac Maharaj, Secretary General of the African National Congress negotiating team
- Roelf Meyer, Chief Negotiator of the National Party talks to end apartheid under F. W. de Klerk, the last leader of white South Africa

Tufts senior Anastasia Konstantakatou described what happened: "We witnessed leading figures of the Apartheid era from different political standpoints discussing Apartheid and democracy in South Africa. We heard about the atrocities committed, about resistance, transition, reconciliation and resilience. Such a discussion was extremely difficult for all the parties involved. . . . Earlier in the semester we had debated whether we should host such a panel; we never expected how important this panel would be for us and for the panelists themselves; we found a neutral and supportive environment to raise issues that elsewhere are taboo."[4]

Asking the Right Questions

Bendetson had an idea: Was there some way that he and others could bring the South African peace brokers together with students, professors, and rival Iraqi combatants to find a way to stop the killing and explore reconciliation? That's when he turned to his former Tufts professor Padraig O'Malley, who lived in South Africa and had written several books on reconciliation. In 1997 O'Malley, a native of Dublin, had orchestrated a private "meeting of the minds" involving the volatile members of Northern Ireland's political parties and former rivals from South Africa's apartheid era. He'd spent nearly two years convincing the Irish leaders to take a chance—to meet with the South Africans to learn whether a reconciliation process could help end the bloodshed in Ireland. Weeks after that conference, a cease-fire was declared in Ireland that opened the door for negotiations that led to the Good Friday Agreement to share power.[5]

It took Teichman and the institute less than a year to organize the Iraq Moving Forward conference, in spite of the challenges of bringing all the players together. O'Malley was integral and indispensable to its outcome and in setting expectations for participants. Bendetson describes O'Malley as "a hero who succeeds because of his tenacity without airs." O'Malley was blunt about what was at stake: "Unless all the parties to the conflict can pull themselves and the communities they represent back from the brink of self-destruction, Iraq will disintegrate. . . . The will to compromise is the key to successful negotiations. Many of our participants learned this the hard way. They believe that by opening Iraqi decision makers to the lessons of their experiences, Iraq may be spared the consequences of pursuing the same routes they once embraced, and find that in the end Iraqis must negotiate with Iraqis."[6]

Held in January 2007, the conference included frank public and private meetings with representatives from Iraq, South Africa, Northern Ireland, and Central America, as well as with professionals and diplomats who had participated in conflict resolution initiatives. Participants heard about the give-and-take required to forge a reconciliation between people who had at one time focused on killing one another. The experience inspired Ali Alawi, the first Iraqi defense minister in the post-Saddam government, to write to the organizers, "To know that there are so many peace-loving intellectuals and friends from around the globe and among those who have gone through traumatic situations is indeed an invaluable experience. Achieving peace requires not only a good intention, but also mastering the art of reconciliation, conflict management and understanding the strengths and weaknesses of rival communities."[7]

No Doesn't Mean *Never*

Hoping to build on the momentum sparked by the conference, Bendetson, O'Malley, and Maharaj met informally with the Iraqis to wish them well on their journey back to Iraq and to learn how they felt about what they'd just experienced. The trio asked the Iraqis what they thought about the idea of taking the reconciliation process to the next level. Initially the Iraqis were reluctant to consider the offer; they seemed concerned about what it would take to get representatives from all the parties together. Bendetson recalled, "Then the Iraqis, O'Malley, and Maharaj paused. They realized that before there could be a larger political reconciliation conference, it would take more time, maybe even six to nine months, before the factions realized that they could not kill all their enemies." O'Malley and Maharaj understood; they had been at that point during the conflicts in their own countries. Bendetson continued, **"We didn't get a red light from the Iraqis; we didn't get a green light—we got no light; we just had a feeling that we could do something that could work."**

Later that evening, during a dinner of brainstorming at Bendetson's home, an ad hoc group of peace brokers was formed. They felt that somehow they could find a way to create a neutral space for these talks to continue. Their goal was to interest a larger number of high-level Iraqis from the Sunni and Shi'a factions in meeting with the South African and Irish reconciliation leaders to explore a similar healing process and move toward peace. Professor O'Malley agreed to go to Iraq in the interim to begin identifying high-level representatives from the Iraqi factions who might be willing to attend a reconciliation conference several months later.

The three prime movers behind the project were Bendetson, who took over project administration and agreed to be the primary underwriter of the initiative; O'Malley, who agreed to be the organizer of a potential reconciliation conference; and Maharaj, who committed to engaging world-class facilitators and finding a neutral host country. Provost Bharucha coordinated the university's support for this unprecedented engagement in what is referred to as "track two" diplomacy—that is, the use of unofficial channels of communication to make progress that can pave the way for subsequent official government efforts. At that time, even official government negotiations in the Iraq war had stalled.

This novel approach to brokering a peace process inspired Finland's former president, Marti Ahtissari, to persuade his country to host the event, which was called Helsinki I. (The following year, he would be awarded the Nobel Peace Prize for three decades of peace initiatives on several continents.)

Entrepreneurs at Work
"This was an entrepreneurial, seat-of-the-pants initiative by highly qualified people who learned to trust one another," Bendetson explained.

> ∾ The type of people who were attracted to this process were people who had a vision of what needed to be

185

done that had never been done before on such a scale. We knew that we could fail, but didn't let that stop us.

Here you have O'Malley, a private citizen, spending months in the middle of a war zone, dedicated to doing whatever it took to make this reconciliation process happen for the Iraqis.

The participants trusted us because we were not stakeholders in the process. The co-conveners were Tufts' Institute of Global Leadership, the University of Massachusetts's John W. McCormack Institute of Public Affairs (Boston), and the Crisis Management Initiative (Helsinki). It was clear to participants and governments that our role was to provide a neutral ground where open conversations could take place— without any person, business, or country receiving financial benefit, political or professional gain. Even though we engaged world-class facilitators and conflict resolution specialists, all of them donated their time to this mission. To me, fostering this kind of forum for world citizenship is a vital role that universities and business leaders can and should play.

Helsinki I was held in September 2007 with Roelf Meyer and Martin McGuinness, deputy prime minister of Northern Ireland, chairing the delegation of facilitators who accompanied them from Northern Ireland and South Africa. They made it clear that this was the Iraqis' meeting and that the agenda was up to them.

Creating a Neutral Zone to Fast-Track Progress

Bendetson took on another role beyond administration and underwriting: the affable and perceptive CEO became a very engaged host at the event. He knew that in such a sensitive situation, it would be important to create a separate informal space where people could relax and get to know one another. Bendetson got permission from the Finnish innkeeper to set up the inn's library to serve as a special room where smoking would be permitted in the normally nonsmoking inn. He knew that in Iraq, relationships were formed in part by men sharing a smoke together. The library became an unlikely yet crucial "comfort zone" where participants formed important bonds and even friendships that would make a difference one year later.

By the third day, the Iraqis asked to see the "Mitchell Accords," which set out the principles for the cease-fire agreements reached to end decades of conflict in Northern Ireland. Then they asked the facilitators to leave the room. "That's when we knew something was happening," Bobby explained. "By the end of the evening they had drafted their own set of reconciliation principles, called their bosses on their cell phones, and then asked us to start setting up Helsinki II, which we held the following year."

Reframing Their Views: From Being Victims to Building a New Alliance

It took only seven months to organize Helsinki II, and to the amazement of Bendetson's ad hoc corps of organizers, thirty-six high-level Sunni, Shi'a, and Kurdish leaders attended. This time Cyril Ramaphosa, former secretary-general of the African National Congress, and McGuinness were coleaders of the facilitating team at the conference, which was once again organized by Professor O'Malley, who had spent nearly a year persuading members of the warring factions to participate in an expanded reconciliation initiative.

Bendetson remembers how he felt as he observed enemies wrestling with the issues, while also taking time to talk to one another privately on walks around the inn's farm. "**I watched as the participants went from being victims of terrorism—on all sides—to building personal relationships and working within a political structure. I was in awe of how they could make the transformation. Pausing—to consider who they once were and who they were now becoming—is a crucial piece of the puzzle in understanding how people can change.**"

Provost Bharucha, who is a cognitive neuroscientist, had come to Helsinki to observe peacemaking outside the laboratory. I asked him what he thought made it possible for longtime enemies to suddenly have a productive dialogue. He explained, "Early on we could tell by their words, their actions, and their body language that the Iraqis were taking over the process and making it their own. They didn't hesitate to have vigorous debate, but at the same time I could see that they were deliberately controlling their urge to react." In an article that he wrote for *Tufts Magazine*, he quoted one participant's comment: "Each of us has thoughts and feelings that could hurt and complicate. But we are here to find agreement and to be positive. So I don't say what's on my mind. I'm trying to find the common ground, the positive, be generous and keep my negative emotions out of it."[8]

The provost explained that the brain has frames—belief systems—through which it quickly sorts and organizes inputs and reactions. In Helsinki, he noticed the way that the facilitators set up conditions and a process to enable the former combatants to find a way through their differences carefully—to pause. Ramaphosa and McGuinness didn't take over the agenda or try to mediate. Instead they respectfully

WHERE ARE WE GOING?

offered possible alternatives when there was a stalemate and gave the sides a chance to "reframe" their views. "Then they eagerly stepped aside, when asked to leave the room by the Iraqi leaders," Bharucha noted, "because the sides made it clear: they were ready to work out their own agreement. That's what they did late into the evening, long past the time we were all supposed to have adjourned."

Accelerating Success by Going Beyond What They Knew

Then the Iraqis surprised everyone when they asked the Helsinki II facilitators for one more favor. Would they be willing to come to Baghdad in three months to craft an agreement on principles for negotiating peace and security as a step toward ending the war? They were, and they volunteered their time once again. When the formal "Withdrawal Agreement" was approved just four months later in late November 2008, several participants wrote Bendetson saying that the Helsinki process had helped get the factions talking and moving forward toward peace.

When I asked Provost Bharucha what he'd learned in Helsinki, he said, "I used to think that education provided you with a set of frameworks to organize what you know in order to guide you for the rest of your life. Now I believe an education needs to give us a framework to keep learning and stretching outside our comfort zones—beyond what we know."

The provost's evolving neurocognitive theory of education encourages us to keep our brains active and growing by "stretching" our minds to consider what we don't know we don't know. This frame of mind is timely, not only for educators but also for managers—whether you are managing (and educating) yourself or leading others. Developing your ability to adjust the lenses through which you see is a powerful way to, as Proust wrote, "to see with fresh eyes."

Interplay of Pause + Curiosity + Humility

Here you had leaders of high rank and reputation—on all sides of three global conflicts—who repeatedly agreed to set aside their fervently held beliefs in service to a mutually beneficial outcome. The three-year process of achieving what few participants (or official diplomats) thought was possible—creating a reconciliation process for the Iraqi people—shows the dynamic interplay of pause, curiosity, and humility. You can also use these practices to produce unimagined results in your everyday ventures—whether making a deal, brokering a solution, or, like Bendetson, running a business.

The experience of shepherding unofficial "track two" citizen-led diplomacy reinforced a belief that Bendetson had long held in his role as a CEO. "**You need to surround yourself in business and in peacemaking with intelligent people who have diverse opinions and aren't afraid to speak up.** Then you need the leadership to facilitate the comments and egos to get to a point where you can take action. You can't get there from here if the leader of a company doesn't have good people or he rules by fear."

As Bobby and I were finishing our interview, he walked me to the door of his office and said softly, "Like my dad told me, most people only get one major 'fork in the road' moment; fortunately I elected to make the choice that I did, and I hope it leads in some small way to less killing."

∞

CHAPTER 13

WHAT'S IN IT FOR ME?

You might be wondering what the stories in Chapter Twelve have to do with you, especially if you don't make your living researching cancer or negotiating peace. If you think about it, however, most of us do come across many of the same types of challenges. As one retired senior executive who negotiated many deals in his day noted, "In their purest form, all challenges are interpersonal. They originate in ignorance or illusion or assumptions about each other's needs and desires."

Think about what you are dealing with these days. At times,

- Do you want to enlist people in your vision when they'd rather just stick with theirs?
- Are you dealing with conflicts that require you to get to the hidden causes of the problem?
- Are you working with people who are reluctant to come to the table to have a conversation?
- Are you managing people who have large egos?

- Are you dealing with miscommunications and faulty assumptions, just as the two doctors were when they were at a stalemate over the perceived difference between immune systems and genetics?

If you are facing situations that are similar to those you saw in these stories, you can see how mastering the Power of Pause practices helps you lead and manage successful collaboration. The next case history demonstrates that it takes mastery to pause—to put yourself in the shoes of your peers, your employees, and your customers—and then persuade them to be early adopters of new ideas.

What's in It for Our Customers and for Us?

> You can have wonderful ideas and passion, but you cannot succeed by doing it alone.
> —MONICA LUECHTEFELD, EXECUTIVE VICE
> PRESIDENT OF SUPPLY CHAIN AND INFORMATION
> TECHNOLOGY, OFFICE DEPOT

Shortly after the 2008 presidential election, technology experts speculated on whether Barack Obama would be able to sustain what had evolved with his campaign's sophisticated use of emerging social networking tools. They termed it the first experiment in "collaborative government."[1] As technologies continue to emerge, often without much warning, it's one thing to get a flash of insight that a new application will dramatically (and inevitably) change the way you and your customers interact, but, as we'll see in the next case history, it's another thing to quickly get the right people on board and to make the right decisions that turn great ideas into profitable realities.

It Has Everything to Do with Alignment

How do you convince people to adopt new ideas ahead of the competition?

That's the challenge and opportunity Monica Luechtefeld faced early in her career at Office Depot, a global office supplies and services company. I first heard her story when she was a guest speaker at the Women on the Move executive education program I was teaching at Florida International University's Center for Leadership. The choices she and her company made at that time made history, and Office Depot is about to become a pioneer once again. It's priorities and practices also provide what I'd call "effectiveness benchmarks" to anyone who wants to get across the finish line, not only having won the race but also having taken your teams and customers with you.

∞

In the early days of the Internet, before businesses realized the impact it would have on commerce, three companies, including Office Depot, were chosen by MIT to participate in a game-changing experiment: developing the first business-to-business e-commerce Web sites. Luechtefeld was put in charge of a project that changed her life and the trajectory of the company's bottom line. Her CEO approved the funding to develop the first Web-based site for ordering office supplies.

It took Luechtefeld's team two years to get the first five hundred businesses connected; by the third year, eleven thousand companies had signed up, then thirty-nine thousand companies. By 2002, online sales had grown to approximately $2 billion; as of 2009, sales exceed $5 billion. When I interviewed Luechtefeld, who in the intervening years had become executive vice president of supply chain and information technology, she was developing Office Depot's next innovation: finding constructive ways for social networking technology to meet the work-life needs of customers increasingly working in virtual work spaces.

As she shared insights culled from experience as a "first mover" and a leader, a checklist of priorities emerged. One overriding concept was key to her organization's success. It's a skill that is required for managers and for anyone who wants an idea to move forward: the skill of collaboration. "To succeed," she explains, "you have to have the skill, talent, and mindset to ask, What don't I know about how my ideas will affect others? Then you go find out the answers and learn how to inspire people to follow you." With that as a platform, here are the principles and practices Luechtefeld shared that may drive first-mover success for you.

Effectiveness Benchmarks

1. *Put customers at the center of whatever you do.* Make sure you put yourselves and those leading the project in the shoes of your customer to better understand how what you are proposing will make life better and simpler for them. ("It's not always the technology experts who can best understand the impact that change has on the end user.")

2. *Work simultaneously from the top down and the bottom up.* Get the backing early on from top management. Then spend most of your time on the front lines helping the people

---

in your company who are closest to the customers understand what you are proposing and doing.

3. *Integrate support systems; don't build silos.* Integrate the way departments, such as customer data systems and call centers, will support and execute the new program. ("We made a significant decision not to create a stand-alone Internet entity, which would have competed against our existing sales structure. It gave us the advantage that other companies missed when their sales staff felt that Internet sales were the enemy.")

4. *Align compensation with strategy.* Help your associates understand the behavior changes that are needed to enable them to succeed when you introduce a game-changing technology or program. If it's strategic, then sales compensation has to change to support the strategic initiative. ("Alignment is everything!")

5. *Provide training, training, and more training.* Customize it for your associates and your customers. ("We spent two years on the road providing Internet training, e-commerce training, and lots of seminars for customers, as well as our associates, many of whom had never used computers, let alone a mouse.")

6. *Be patient, but be an evangelist!* Enrolling people (colleagues and customers) in moving from the old ways of doing things to the new ways can take longer than you think. ("It doesn't matter how good you are at seeing the future; you have to hit the road and be an evangelist for your idea.")

7. *Leverage what you know, and learn what you don't know.* To succeed in a matrix organization, you have to know how your ideas can potentially affect other departments and divisions. Collaboration and communication are everything, and they start at the top. ("We operate today with a 'shared leadership' model. When you propose a new idea, the first question you get from our CEO is, Have you talked to 'so and so' and if not, well then, come back when you have.")

Luechtefeld's comments motivated me to revisit the company's Web site to learn more about its values. That's where I came across these words under the Worklife heading: "We share the desire to maximize human potential to achieve personal dreams."[2] Taking a few moments to "maximize human potential" is more important than ever today. Based in the principles of positive psychology, this approach toward professional development is emerging as a powerful new management tool that is the focus of extensive research at the University of Michigan Ross School of Business. The research, along with that presented in Marcus Buckingham's book *Now, Discover Your Strengths*, argues that the best way to motivate people is to focus on building their strengths rather than improving weaknesses.[3]

In teaching senior managers the strengths-based approach to professional development, I realized that it takes introspection—a pause—to consider how to manage around your weakness, do a better job building on your strengths, and then do the same for others. In Chapter Fourteen you'll find specific and timely ways to practice an invaluable skill to help people be their best.

CHAPTER 14

APPRECIATIONS

THE POWER OF PAUSE IN ACTION

How *do* you maximize human potential? You provide effective, timely appreciation. In this case, I'm not talking about a bonus, a raise, a gift certificate, extra time off, advanced training, or other well-deserved perks that are important ways to reward performance. I'm talking about taking a few minutes to let someone know specifically what he or she did that made a difference.

POWER OF PAUSE PRACTICE #12:
Strengthen Relationships: Offer Timely, Specific Appreciation

Ask yourself, *When was the last time I felt genuinely appreciated?*

One thing you, your colleagues, your customers, your family, and the other important people in your life can never get enough of is appreciation. Appreciation *doesn't* mean that you endorse someone's behavior or opinion. It simply means that you are pausing to honor, notice, and recognize another person. You can even deeply appreciate a difference of opinion, which is an important opportunity to build trust in any relationship.

In today's business world, we often feel that we barely have time to think, let alone to appreciate someone or ourselves. **While we're busy trying to motivate people and lead them, there's one thing we can easily undervalue and overlook: appreciation is motivating.**

Whether we're meeting face-to-face; through a videoconference, teleconference, or telepresence; or on the Internet, it's easy to dive in, get our agenda started, and begin batting ideas back and forth. Maybe we think we are productive because we get right down to business. At the same time, maybe we're feeling pressed to generate more ideas or more money, to hire more people or seek more opportunities. If that's the case, we're trying to produce "more" based on the assumption that we don't have enough time, money, people, resources, or fresh ideas. In a way, it's as if we're running on a tank that's "nearly empty"—fueling our attempt to do our best from a mindset of scarcity.

Instead, if you would first take a moment to verbally or even mentally appreciate something about someone else or yourself, then you would be launching your conversation, meeting, or phone call from an outlook of abundance rather than scarcity. When you start out with an attitude of abundance, it can make all the difference in how you will relate to others over the next minutes or hours. That's what clients have found when they put "Appreciations" at the top of their meeting agenda. Here's one of their stories. It's typical of what others have found happens when they discover, as we learned in Part One of this book, that the mindset you start with really does affect where you end up.

Un- Be- Lievable!

How do you start off on the right foot when you'd rather run than walk?

∞

Joe Meunier was the head of operations at an international transportation brokerage company where he'd worked since high school. He was a street-smart local-boy-made-good who'd started out handling freight on the loading dock. The company handled airfreight, shipping, customs, and security arrangements for such products as multimillion-dollar computers and high-security screening equipment for foreign embassies. I'd been hired by the company's owners to help the top executives and department heads work better together. Their employees were operating on overload. Trust me when I tell you this: they were by no means a "touchy-feely" group!

Each person was dedicated to getting his or her deadline-driven, detail-oriented jobs done. However, there wasn't much of a sense of teamwork or a feeling of respect. This showed up in many ways, such as meetings rarely starting on time because people, especially senior management, would come late. I asked them to try an experiment—to change the way they started *any* meeting. I explained the new quick-start process: "Please take a total of a few minutes to let each person answer this question in one or two sentences, max: What's one thing you appreciate about yourself, someone in the room, or someone outside the room? And here's the rule: no comments, no attempts to agree with or fix them; just listen to each other's appreciation for anything at all—whether it's large or small."

I wish you could have been there to see the looks of incredulity on their faces: We have no time for this! Nevertheless, they started running their meetings this way, and before long, people were coming to meetings early. Tempers didn't flare as quickly when the agenda got to tough topics and uncomfortable decisions. People moved through their agenda faster and got more done, partly because they were more willing to listen and to try to understand what someone meant, not just react to what they thought someone said *or* implied. Soon they developed their own "Can Do" team program that led to faster, better ways to get their work done—even when a recession hit and they had their first-ever layoffs.

Their success didn't end at the warehouse; it also showed up months later at a meeting with nearly twenty vendors, customers, airline reps, and government regulators. A lot was at stake because there was a dispute over freight shipping regulations, security, and local port authority fees and policies. There was no time to waste with people on edge and deadlines to meet. That's when Joe Meunier decided to take a risk. He'd run meetings like this before and knew that people could get angry and just walk out.

Joe opened the meeting saying, "Today I'd like to ask each of you to trust me about a different way for us to get started. It's something we've been doing at our company. Believe me, we thought it was nuts at first. But it has made a heck of a difference in how we get our work done—and it only takes a few minutes. We'll just go around the room and answer in one sentence, What's one thing you appreciate about yourself, someone in the room, or someone outside the room? Then we'll move on to the rest of our meeting."

As a no-nonsense leader, Joe had a reputation to protect. He'd weathered a lot of storms in his years of negotiating tough deals with the people in the room. After the meeting, he called to tell me what happened. "It was *unbelievable!* All we did was start with the appreciations practice, and after that the energy in the room completely changed. People *knew* each other, yeah, we've all been in the trenches and we've even socialized, but suddenly it's like we *saw* each other differently. We worked things through in ways I never could have imagined. And it took less time than we'd scheduled."

∞

Other clients who have put the appreciations practice to work include CEOs, universities, Young Presidents Organization Forum members, unions, television stations, banks, and yes, the (formerly) dysfunctional hotel employees (whom we met in Part Three) who had been blaming one another for things that went wrong in their race to raise rankings. Most admit that the only problem they've run into is that on days when they think they don't have time to start meetings with a quick round of appreciations, the meetings take longer and are less productive. Why? One client says it's because "We weren't connected to begin with; then we kick ourselves and realize that the thing that we think we don't have time for—relating—is exactly what we need to do in order to succeed."

It's no secret that you benefit from practices that build trust—especially when you are short on time or don't know

THE POWER OF PAUSE

one another that well. (There are tips on effective appreciation following this chapter.) The time it takes to appreciate someone in this way is less than the time it takes to draw a deep breath and let it out. Try it for yourself. Once you have mastered this practice, you'll have an important advantage when you're called to manage yourself or others or a team — no matter what curve balls come your way.

The Power of Pause: Putting It All Together When Everything Is on the Line

Being able to sincerely appreciate and respect the people you work with is also part of the Effectiveness Equation:

**Pause (Presence) + Curiosity + Humility =
Professional Effectiveness and Personal Fulfillment**

In this final story, you will see a manager combine the discipline of pausing, to avoid snap decisions despite public pressure; the mindset of curiosity, to cultivate talent and give people the benefit of the doubt; and an extra measure of humility, to inspire his team to achieve extraordinary results even when the odds are against them.

Perfect Balance: The Story of a World Championship Manager

What do cribbage, respect, and humility have to do with winning against the odds?

What can we learn from a world-class manager who is admired by his players, his peers, his bosses, his competitors, and his organization's fanatical customers? This final story lets us see how the soft-spoken manager of a championship team drives performance in difficult times. How does he do it? He takes the time to reflect, to get curious about his options, and to find the perfect balance between his self-respect and faith in his players. Then he makes the tough calls with humility—especially when the heat is on.

∞

"Nice Guys Finish First" was the title of a column in the *New York Times* written by Doug Glanville, a former player for the New York Yankees. He wasn't talking about a Yankee team member; he was referring to Terry Francona, the coach of the Yankees' long time rival, the Boston Red Sox. Francona had been his coach when Glanville had played for the Philadelphia Phillies several years earlier. "Under his tutelage I played the best baseball of my career, and I owe a lot to the environment he created in the locker room."[1]

A Scheduled Pause Opens Doors

It's no secret that today many of us feel that it's harder to get to know our coworkers and to foster a supportive environment when we need it most. It's no different in baseball, with players' demanding schedules leaving little time for family and little time off during the season. That's why it's intriguing to learn that one of the pregame locker room routines Francona practices is to play an intensely competitive game of cribbage with his players, including one of his rookies, Dustin "Pedey" Pedroia. He explains that he arrives at a ballpark early, "so that I can do all my prep work before the first player arrives. Then, if they want to come in and play, I have the time. . . . When Dustin Pedroia was struggling, he knew he could come in here, play cribbage, talk about things, and relieve the pressure."[2]

When Pedroia hit a batting slump in the 2008 American League Championship Series (ALCS) playoff games, Francona understood that this scrappy young player, whom many had doubted when he first came to the team, needed to find his way out of the slump on his own. At the end of the season, the twenty-five-year-old, five-foot-seven second baseman was named the American League's Most Valuable Player. This recognition came after playing only two seasons in the major leagues, with Francona quietly standing behind him time and again.

Benefit of the Doubt Builds Trust

What is the role of managers—in baseball and in the workplace of today? Their deliverables aren't that different. One top priority is finding and nurturing the best talent and keeping them motivated to do their best work as individuals and as a team. That's what Terry Francona has mastered. Baseball experts will tell you that there are managers who call the shots by the book: the statistics and the game plan. There are others who go with their gut. But Francona is recognized as exceptionally skilled in genuinely understanding each player—how to weigh when to push him and when to pull back, and how to support him when he hits a dreaded slump. Glanville talked about Francona's approach to meeting the bottom line: "His top concern was how we went about our business to achieve this bottom line. If we did it honorably, he had nothing but words of encouragement for us."[3]

Terry Francona has taught me a lot about making the tough calls; those are lessons I don't hesitate to pass along to my coaching clients. One of the trickiest calls he makes comes when he decides to shake up the batting order because a player is repeatedly struggling at the plate. One night, after giving his leadoff player several weeks to get back on track, Francona had him hit lower in the batting order (a less prestigious assignment). That's when the player finally hit his way out of a long batting slump. I shared this story with a successful senior executive. He was furious about being temporarily shifted to another (less prestigious) assignment. I explained, "Maybe, like Francona, your boss is just saying you need a break and a change in the lineup." There was total silence at the other end of the line as this loyal rainmaker paused to consider a different way of seeing why he'd been relocated. He later was promoted to executive vice president after getting a much-needed opportunity to develop experience, perspective, and patience.

Humility and a Measured Pause Leverage Talent

There is another aspect to the position that a manager plays; it has to do with weighing the ramifications of his decisions. His choices reflect how he juggles the often fragile egos of his top talent while also answering to the expectations of the other players, his staff, the customers, his bosses, the investors, and the media. Being second-guessed is a given in baseball, and it's not an unfamiliar situation to face in business either. Baseball is a business where success also depends on leaders who have the skill and the humility of a diplomat.

"It was a tough thing to swallow and have to deal with, but it is what it is." Those were the words that the Red Sox team captain and catcher, Jason Veritek, spoke after Game 5 of the 2008 ALCS playoffs when Francona sent in a pinch hitter for him for the first time in his storied career. Veritek had been in a batting

THE POWER OF PAUSE

slump for several months. His manager had been reluctant to show any disrespect for the captain, an All Star catcher and two-time winner of the World Series who had caught a record one thousand Red Sox games. Earlier in the regular season, there was speculation about how Francona would manage the situation. *Boston Globe* reporter Tony Massarotti had written, "Francona believes in the greater good of his team, of giving proven veterans the respect they deserve, and hitting for Varitek, he argued, would pierce the very essence of his team."[4]

But then came the ALCS playoffs, and everything was on the line. The pinch hitter took Veritek's place in Game 5. However, the next night Veritek redeemed himself by hitting a tie-breaking home run in the sixth inning of Game 6, forcing a seventh game and giving the Sox a chance to win the final game in the ALCS.

In the final game of the series, only one Red Sox batter connected for a hit, and the team lost the game to the Tampa Bay Rays, 3–1. Veritek wasn't the only hitter who struck out swinging; at the same time, the Sox pitchers couldn't find their zone, and the Rays' pitchers couldn't miss. Not surprisingly, Red Sox Nation was stunned and disappointed at the loss. However, it was extraordinary to see a number of favorable Internet postings from loyal fans, who rarely hesitate to second-guess the outcome of a game. Instead, like the manager, they expressed their appreciation—giving the injured and struggling players credit for pushing their limits—right up to the last at-bat.

Positioning the Team to Win

You might be wondering why I would share a clip from a manager's record that doesn't feature a big win. That's the thing I admire most about Terry Francona: he's focused on winning, but winning isn't the only thing that matters. Yes, of course he is competitive, and he will fight for what he believes is right—for his players and for the love of the game. As AP sportswriter Howard Ulman points out, "His .710 winning percentage (22–9) postseason games is the best in major league history among managers with at least 20 games. He also has the most World Series wins (eight) without a loss."[5]

In my eyes, what sets Terry Francona apart as a world-class manager is that no matter what odds or frustrating last-minute changes he faces, he does his best to position his team to always have the opportunity to win. You hear it in the way he treats his players—with respect, honesty, and a sense of humor. You see it in the way he trusts his coaches. You hear it when you listen to him handle the postgame press conferences. With his candid, authentic, self-deprecating manner, he balances accountability for the judgment calls he made and gives credit to those who did well. He doesn't miss a chance to express faith in those he knows *can* still do well in days to come, regardless of how they played that day.

∞

The focus of this book has been about how to play the game to position yourself and others for an opportunity to win. As in sports, you don't always win. But if you play the game well, you are always positioned for a better chance to win. The way I see it, if more of us could show up at work with the attitude of Terry Francona, we'd have a team and "fans" behind us who could transform success into a winning legacy.

TIPS FOR EFFECTIVELY GIVING AND ACCEPTING APPRECIATION

The practice of appreciation is a powerful pause. It shows that you are choosing to disengage the clutch momentarily so as to engage more effectively (with yourself or others) without losing sight of what still needs to be done when, moments later, you race ahead.

❧ *Practice humility.* It takes humility to offer appreciation as well as to accept it. Many times we focus on what's not being done right—we're critical of ourselves or others. Taking a step back gives you and others a valuable perspective when you openly let others see you value learning lessons from what's working and what's not working. We saw the power of this type of pause at work in the earlier stories about the bankers, a dean, a marketing manager, and a lieutenant colonel.

❧ *Be specific.* One way to make appreciation count is to be specific about why you are recognizing someone. The more specific you are, the harder it is for her to deflect your recognition, because the specificity makes what you are saying more believable. Well-intended but vague comments such as "You did a great job" or "I really appreciate you" are so general that it's hard for someone to know what he did that mattered to you. Instead you could say, "Your presentation was very good yesterday because you were concise, you engaged the client, and you gave them examples of how we could help them get faster results than they initially expected."

❧ *Provide timely performance feedback.* One of the most important opportunities to provide appreciation is with timely and balanced assessments or a performance review. It's crucial to let someone know specifically how her work has made a difference and to clarify what it will take to advance her career. Yum Brands CEO, David Novak, says that *great* leaders take an interest in their people, "People are starved for direct feedback. People want to hear how they can do better. Too many leaders don't provide that feedback."[1] He says he begins his feedback with a specific appreciation followed by a suggestion (not a "but") for how employees can be even more effective.

❧ *Little things count.* Appreciation doesn't have to wait for something big to happen. In addition to being as specific as possible about what you appreciate, try to be timely with your comment. You don't have to wait for your next meeting, newsletter, or recognition event.

❧ *Pause when someone deflects your appreciation.* She may say, "Oh, it was nothing" or "No problem." Maybe you do that yourself when someone compliments or thanks you. When people deflect your praise, consider why it may be uncomfortable for them to accept acknowledgment. You can thoughtfully say, "It seems that it's not easy for you to accept this attention. I'm sure you have your reasons."

Then just listen. Or you may take a lighthearted approach and say, "OK, I know you like to work hard and that you don't feel what you did is a big deal. Would you do me a favor? Just say 'Thank you.'" You may laugh, and the point is made: it's OK for you to let her know that what she did mattered to you (or others), and it's OK if she is uncomfortable about it. She understands your sincere intention and that you meant what you said.

❧ *Get curious.* If you are the recipient of a "good job" comment that leaves you wondering what you did that was worth recognition, get curious. Try saying something like, "Thank you; I appreciate that. Could you do me a favor? Either now or some other time, could you let me know what it was that I did that makes you say that? I could guess, but I might not really know what mattered to you."

CHAPTER 15

THE POWER OF PAUSE PRACTICES

TWELVE WAYS TO BE YOUR BEST AND TO SUCCEED IN A DEMANDING, 24/7 WORLD

op athletes and star performers know it takes practice to be their best—whether it's perfecting a pitch, hitting the right note, or changing their previous formula for success. You, too, can play the way you practice—working with colleagues and coaches to put what you've learned in this book adeptly into play. At the same time, researchers encourage us to preserve an agile mind by continually exercising and stretching our brains. With practice, you *can* develop new neural pathways and habits that become second nature, even if at first they feel counterintuitive. There is power in even a single brief pause, and that strength is yours to tap.

This summary offers a quick way to be your best, no matter who or what shows up in your day. These practices are doubly important as a means of preempting the possibility of being misunderstood—especially in fast-moving situations or when using text messaging, e-mails, or forums where the lack of verbal or visual cues can trigger missed understandings and false solutions.

211

The Power of Pause Practices

1. *Drive Your Choices Instead of Being Driven*
   Apply the Power of Pause process to take back self-control and recognize you always have a choice: disengage the clutch, ease off the accelerator (and back off of your assumptions), and pause before shifting gears to take control of your reactions. Use a pause to regain presence of mind and uncover better, less obvious options.

2. *Be Aware of Your Filters (and Theirs)*
   Remember that filters can lead to unconscious misinterpretations.

3. *Give the Benefit of the Doubt*
   Check your assumptions. Meaning isn't in the words: it's in the *interpretation* of them—by you and by others. When in doubt, ask, "Can you help me see what you see?"

4. *Stop Putting Deposits in Your Resentment Bank Account*
   Resist jumping to premature conclusions or depositing frustrations based on your perception of "the facts."

5. *Use Rephrasing as a Twenty-First-Century Risk Management Tool*
   Stick your neck out: rephrase what you *think* someone meant by what he said; it builds trust, especially if he needs to clarify your interpretation or add more information.

6. *Use the Get Curious Not Furious Approach*
   "Missed understandings" happen—a lot! They're normal. Try not to take them personally. Use the Curiosity Checklist to gauge how open you or someone else may be to another perspective.

7. *Ask: What's on Your Plate?*
   Understand someone else's priorities while you *also*
   acknowledge your own. Remember to ask yourself, *What's
   on my plate?*

8. *Ask: What Don't I Know I Don't Know?*
   In order to drive success with an extra measure of humility,
   ask, *What don't I know I don't know?* about what's driving
   me or them or the situation? Ask, *What don't they know
   they don't know?* about themselves or me or the situation?

9. *Take Responsibility for Being Understood: Reverse Rephrase*
   Reverse rephrase to confirm that you were understood; welcome the chance to clear up any "missed understandings."

10. *Make Withdrawals from Your Resentment Bank Account*
    Withdraw earlier deposits to prevent them from building
    up negative energy in your account. Rethink your assump-
    tions about a person or about a situation that didn't turn
    out the way you expected; be alert for hidden opportunities
    to uncover an unimaginably better solution.

11. *Know Your Trigger Points (and Theirs)*
    Prevent yourself or others from being caught in self-defeating
    patterns. Become aware of who or what triggers you so
    that you can respond instead of react.

12. *Strengthen Relationships: Offer Timely, Specific Appreciation*
    Put the Power of Pause in action with timely, specific
    recognition of what works and why. Help people also
    know what they can do to be even more effective and
    how you can support them in being their best.

IT'S TIME

NOW IT'S UP TO YOU

How can we do our best work in a fast-changing world today and be even better prepared to make a difference in a future we're trying to imagine?

In the beginning, I invited you to consider the power of a pause. The times when we least think we have the time to take a time-out are the times we need it most. That's what we heard when the nurse simply realized, *You mean all I have to do is take a breath?* That's what we saw when Bobby Bendetson didn't listen to people telling him, "It's not for you to be a peacemaker; leave it to the experts." Instead, he paused to reflect, *Well, maybe you're right, but let's just see what we can do.*

So what are the tools at your fingertips now? You have your voice, the choice, and the ability to develop new habits that will enable you to *do well with less stress.* That is the reality: you can learn new ways of being your best and feel that what you did mattered. It's not just whether you cross the finish line first, but as Dr. Carbone demonstrated, it's whether you bring the rest of the team with you.

Teamwork and collaboration can be messy. Some people aren't always open to new ideas even when they say they are open-minded. Those are times when you can practice the Power of Pause—to formulate a response, not give in to your reaction to theirs. At other times you'll be on automatic and feel that you just can't take the time to listen to others. That's when you will be better able to hear someone else say, "Can we take a moment just to make sure we have no other option at this time?" Or, like Lieutenant Colonel Moore in the heat of battle, you will mentally disengage to ask, *What's happening, what's not happening, and what can I do to change the outcome?* That's what pitcher Jonathan Papelbon did after losing the game but before returning to the field to answer the hungry media. It was a question that he had to answer first for himself—then he went back to winning games.

Whichever stories in this book appealed to you, whatever lessons you learned, it's my hope you will put them to work as opportunities present themselves. Be patient as you move up the learning curve from awareness to action. Let people know that you are trying out some new ideas. Progress may come from simply becoming aware that you could have paused. Over time it will become second nature.

Now it's time to take a moment to ask, *What do we see in our future?*

Virtualization—the capacity to work anywhere with anyone at any time—and globalization are changing the way we work and with whom we work. I never imagined that I would be teaching these Power of Pause practices across continents and hemispheres while the ideas were being translated (and rephrased) into over a dozen languages. As I watch people put the practices to work regardless of their profession or culture, it is humbling to realize that the pressures to respond to time compression, fractured attention spans, and constant change don't stop at anyone's borders. It is inspiring to discover that people of many cultures share an urgent curiosity to reclaim *the right to pause*. I wrote this book to help you take back your voice, restore your choice, and make positive change.

The Power of Pause practices never go out of style—especially today when we're expected to do so much under extreme pressure and do it right, on the spot. **It's time to stop turning against each other and turn things around, with each of us playing our part.** The principles in this book have worked for me and for colleagues, clients, family, friends, and audiences—and they will work for you.

I've given you twelve practices and three short phrases to enable you to be your best no matter what comes your way at work each day:

The Power of Pause
Get Curious Not Furious
What Don't I Know I Don't Know?

Before you know it, you will recall one of these phrases, and it will transform the way you see a situation and enable you to achieve a better outcome.

For years I've received e-mails, phone calls, or comments like this one: "You'll never believe what happened the other day when a client got furious with his boss and was ready to quit. I calmly suggested he take a minute to consider, 'What don't you know you don't know about what's going on for *him*?' That one question helped the client turn the situation around, from a near breakdown to a break-through—in about five minutes." He kept his client from having a Wile E. Coyote moment.

Yes, you can choose to pause and make minutes count.

You now know how to make a pause powerful—for yourself and for others.

You will have more impact and make wiser choices because you won't be held hostage to your reactions or the reactions of others.

And if you want to put yourself in a position to win, and to feel that you've done your best work no matter what comes at you in fast-changing times, these practices aren't optional—they're indispensable.

It's time to take back your voice, restore your choice, and make positive change.

At the beginning I offered you an invitation: to explore whether there is a better way for you to be your best and to feel that you made a difference, regardless of what is going on around you. You've reached the end of this book, but hardly the end of your journey. Your next step is here. Start starting.

NOTES

An Invitation to the Power of Pause

1. Linda Stone, "Linda Stone's Thoughts on Attention and Specifically, Continuous Partial Attention," http://www.lindastone. net. A former Microsoft and Apple Computer executive, Stone coined the term *continuous partial attention* as a result of her research on the impact of computing technology on its users. "To pay continuous partial attention is to pay partial attention—CONTINUOUSLY. . . . We want to effectively scan for opportunity and optimize for the best opportunities, activities, and contacts, in any given moment. . . . It is an always-on, anywhere, anytime, anyplace behavior that involves an artificial sense of constant crisis."

2. Mark Bittman, "I Need a Virtual Break. No, Really," *New York Times*, March 2, 2008, http://www.nytimes.com/2008/03/02/ fashion/02sabbath.html. Bittman reports on how the idea of temporarily unplugging from 24/7 access to electronic technology emerged in blog postings, and what happened to people when they turned off the "always on" switch.

Chapter Two

1. "Looking Ahead: Implications of the Present," *Harvard Business Review*, September-October 1997, 18. This seventy-fifth-anniversary cover story featured the forecasts of Peter Drucker, Esther Dyson, Charles Handy, Paul Saffo, and Peter Senge.

2. Lieutenant Colonel Harold Moore, "After Action Report," http://www.lzxray.com/documents/aar-xray.pdf.

3. Lieutenant General Harold Moore (Ret.), "Battlefield Leadership," http://www.lzxray.com/battle.htm.

4. Herbert Benson, "Are You Working Too Hard?" *Harvard Business Review*, November 2005, 54–56.

Chapter Three

1. William Ury, *The Power of a Positive No* (New York: Bantam, 2007), 147–151.
2. Robert Bolton, *People Skills: How to Assert Yourself, Listen to Others and Resolve Conflicts* (New York: Touchstone, 1986), 34.
3. "Who's on First?" is the comedy wordplay routine Bud Abbott and Lou Costello first performed in their 1930s radio broadcasts. To read or listen to the routine, go to http://www .baseball-almanac.com/humor4.shtml.

Tips and *Yeah, Buts*

1. Viktor Frankl, *Man's Search for Meaning*, rev. ed. (1984; repr. New York: Simon & Schuster, 1959), 86.
2. Thomas Crook, "Snooze It or Lose It," *Prevention Magazine*, May 2008, http://www.prevention.com/cda/article/snooze-it-or-lose-it.
3. Stefan Klein, "Time Out of Mind," trans. S. Frisch, *New York Times*, March 3, 2008, A19. Klein is the author of *The Secret Pulse of Time: Making Sense of Life's Scarcest Commodity* (New York: Da Capo Press, 2007).

Chapter Four

1. This principle is advanced by Jan Smith, founder of the Center for Authentic Leadership. She has taught thousands of professionals "future thinking" leadership practices. Her teachings incorporate insights she gained while working with Fernando Flores and Ken Anbender, both global pioneers in communication dynamics.
2. Baba Shiv, Ziv Carmon, and Dan Ariely, "Placebo Effects of Marketing Actions: Consumers May Get What They Pay For," *Journal of Marketing Research* 42 (November 2005): 383–393.
3. Jonah Lehrer, *Boston Globe*, October 5, 2008, K1. See also *How We Decide* (New York, Houghton Mifflin, 2009).

4. Jenny Anderson and Charles Duhigg, "Flirting with Disaster," *New York Times*, September 21, 2008, B10, http://www .nytimes.com/2008/09/21/business/21exec.html.

5. Jennifer Whitson and Adam Galinsky, "Lacking Control Increases Illusory Pattern Perception," *Science* 3 (October 2008): 115–117. This research focused on the possible causes for irrational behavior when people feel that things are out of control.

6. "Want Hypertension? Hurry Up!" *Cardiology Online*, November 20, 2002, http://www.cardiologyonline.com/ journal_articles/Want.htm. See also Lijing L. Yan, "The Psychosocial Factors and Risk of Hypertension," *Journal of the American Medical Association* 290, no.16 (October 22, 2003), http://jama.ama-assn.org/cgi/content/abstract/290/16/21. See also Bill Weir, "Efficiency Overload: Why Demanding More May Be Wearing Us Thin," ABC News, May 8, 2008, http:// abcnews.go.com/Business/story?id=4813441&page=1.

7. Malcolm Gladwell, *Blink* (New York: Little, Brown, 2005), 233.

8. Linda Stone, "Just Breathe: Building the Case for Email Apnea," blog posting, February 8, 2008, http://www .huffingtonpost.com/linda-stone/just-breathe-building-th_b_ 85651.html.

9. Edward Hallowell and John Ratey, *Delivered from Distraction* (New York: Ballantine Books, 2006), 156–159.

10. Jonathan Clements, "What We Want to Hear Drowns Out the Rest," *Wall Street Journal*, April 8, 2007, A3.

11. Mark L. Knapp and Judith A. Hall, *Nonverbal Communication in Human Interaction* (Belmont, Calif.: Wadsworth, 2005), 13.

Chapter Five

1. Robert Bolton, *People Skills: How to Assert Yourself, Listen to Others and Resolve Conflicts* (New York: Touchstone, 1986), 34.

2. John Naisbitt, *Megatrends* (New York: Warner Books, 1982); see also John Naisbitt, *High Tech, High Touch* (London: Nicholas Brealey, 2001).

Chapter Six

1. Janet Rae-Dupree, "Can You Become a Creature of New Habits?" *New York Times,* May 4, 2008, www.nytimes.com/2008/05/04/business/04unbox.html. See also Dawna Markova, *The Open Mind* (San Francisco: Conari Press, 1996).

Chapter Seven

1. Jerome Groopman, *How Doctors Think* (Boston: Mariner Books, 2008), 24, 35, and 65.
2. Larry Olmstead, "Service Agreement," *Arrive* (Amtrak magazine), January-February 2008, 23. See also Kirk Kazanjian, *Exceeding Customer Expectations* (New York, Broadway Business, 2007).
3. Charles Tilly, *Credit and Blame* (Princeton, N.J.: Princeton University Press, 2008), 35–36.
4. Nance Guilmartin, *Healing Conversations: What to Say When You Don't Know What to Say* (San Francisco: Jossey-Bass, 2002), 122.
5. Joe Nocera, "Put Buyers First? What a Concept," *New York Times,* January 5, 2008, B1.

Chapter Eight

1. Jerry Remy and Don Orsillo, New England Sports Network, broadcast coverage, May 9, 2008.
2. Nick Cafardo, "Papelbon Entering an Entirely Different Zone," *Boston Globe,* May 10, 2008, D1.

Tips and *Yeah, Buts*

1. Robert Cialdini and Steve Martin, "The Power of Persuasion," *Training Journal,* December 2006, 40.
2. Mark Matousek, "Stroke of Luck," *AARP Magazine,* November–December 2008, 28. See also Jill Bolte Taylor's book, *My Stroke of Luck* (New York: Viking, 2008).

Chapter Nine

1. "Looking Ahead: Implications of the Present," *Harvard Business Review,* September-October 1997, 18.

2. David Garvin and Michael A. Roberto, "What You Don't Know About Making Decisions," *Harvard Business Review*, September 2001, 4, 7.
3. Homer-Dixon quoted in Barry Boyce, "Complexity, Chaos and Collapse: Why We Need New Ways of Thinking," *Shambhala*, September 2008, 46–47.
4. Gary Small and Gigi Vorgan, "Meet Your iBrain," *Scientific American Mind*, October–November 2008, 47.
5. Daniel Goleman, *Social Intelligence: The New Science of Human Relationships* (New York: Bantam, 2006-7), 40–44. See also "The Biology of Leadership," *Harvard Business Review*, September 2008, 3.

Chapter Ten
1. Jim Collins, *Good to Great* (New York: HarperCollins, 2001), 20–21.

Chapter Eleven
1. Sarah Kershaw, "My Other Family Is the Office," *New York Times*, December 4, 2008, E7.

Tips and *Yeah, Buts*
1. Pema Chodron, "The Answer to Aggression and Anger Is Patience," *Shambhala*, March 2005, http://www.shambhalasun.com/index.php?option=com_content&task=view&id=1309 & Itemid=247. Chodron helps readers apply patience and curiosity to understand the causes of aggression and to stop the repeating patterns that lead to anger, resentment, and suffering.
2. Nance Guilmartin, *Healing Conversations: What to Say When You Don't Know What to Say* (San Francisco: Jossey-Bass, 2002), 271.
3. Bryan Marquard, "Oliver G. Selfridge, Student of the Mind," *Boston Globe*, December 14, 2008, B5.

Chapter Twelve

1. John P. Walsh and Nancy G. Maloney, "Collaboration Structure, Communication Media, and Problems in Scientific Work Teams," *Journal of Computer-Mediated Communication* 12, no. 2 (2007), http://jcmc.indiana.edu/vol12/issue2/walsh.html. John Toon, "Won't You Be My Neighbor?" *Horizons Research*, Summer 2007, http://gtresearchnews.gatech.edu/reshor/rh-s07/neighbor.htm.

2. Heather Wax, "Cooperation Counts for Math Professor," *Boston Globe*, October 15, 2007, http://www.boston.com/yourlife/health/articles/2007/10/15/cooperation_counts_for_math_professor/.

3. In AACR's announcement of the Landon-AACR Innovator Award for International Collaboration in Cancer Research, CEO Margaret Foti underscored its importance: "To ensure continued progress in conquering cancer, researchers must be willing to share resources and technologies, lend expertise, and communicate new concepts, perspectives and methodologies to the worldwide cancer community." Dr. Carbone's team included Hainig Yang, Ph.D., University of Hawaii; Nancy Cox, Ph.D., and Ian Steele, Ph.D., University of Chicago; Harvey Pass, M.D., NYU School of Medicine and Clinical Cancer Center; Joseph Testa, Ph.D., Fox Chase Cancer Center; Y. Izzetin Baris, M.D., University of Hacettepe, Ankara, Turkey; A. Umran Dogan, Ph.D., University of Iowa; and Salih Emri, M.D., and Murat Tuncer, M.D., Hacettepe University School of Medicine, Ankara, Turkey. See http://www.aacr.org/.

4. Konstantakatou quoted in "Background: The Progression from Tufts University to Baghdad," www.tuftsgloballeadership.org/files/resources/iraq_progression.pdf, 2. For more information, see the 2005–2006 annual report of the Tufts Institute of Global Leadership, http://www.tuftsgloballeadership.org/files/resources/igl0506ar.pdf, 10.

5. Margaret Bucholt, "A Gatherer of Minds," *UMass Boston* 6, no. 1 (Winter/Spring 2002); available at http://www.

omalley.co.za/NXT/gateway.dll?f=templates&fn=default. htm$vid=Omalley:OmalleyView&npusername=OmalleyUs er&nppassword=OmalleyPass.

6. "Iraq Moving Forward," internal overview document, Institute for Global Leadership, Tufts University, 1.
7. "Background," 5.
8. Jamshed Bharucha, "In Helsinki, a Meeting of the Minds," *Tufts Magazine*, Summer 2008, 10.

Chapter Thirteen

1. Sheryl Stolberg, "A Rewired Bully Pulpit: Big, Bold and Unproven," Week in Review, *New York Times*, November 23, 2008; David Carr, "Obama's Personal Linked In," *New York Times*, November 10, 2008, B1; David Talbot, "How Obama *Really* Did It," *Technology Review*, September–October 2008, www.technologyreview.com/web/21222/.
2. Office Depot, "Our Values," http://www.officedepot.com/ specialLinks.do?file5/companyinfo/companyfacts/ourvalues. jsp&template=companyinfo.
3. University of Michigan Ross School of Business, "Reflected Best Self," http://www.bus.umich.edu/Positive/POS-Teaching-and-Learning/ReflectedBestSelfExercise.html; Marcus Buckingham, *Now, Discover Your Strengths* (New York: Free Press, 2001).

Chapter Fourteen

1. Doug Glanville, "Nice Guys Finish First," *New York Times*, October 15, 2008, http://www.nytimes.com/2008/10/15/ opinion/15glanville.html.
2. Steve Wulf, "Terry Francona," *ESPN: The Magazine*, September 11, 2008, http://sports.espn.go.com/espnmag/ story?id=3582284.
3. Glanville, "Nice Guys Finish First."
4. Tony Massarotti, "Veritek Feels Pinch, Doesn't Flinch," *Boston Globe*, October 8, 2008, C5.

5. Howard Ulman, "Boston Manager Terry Francona Gets Three-Year Extension," *USA Today*, February 24, 2008, http://www.usatoday.com/sports/baseball/2008-02-24-2145456500_x.htm.

Tips

1. Adam Bryant, "At Yum Brands, Rewards for Good Work," *New York Times*, July 11, 2009, http://www.nytimes.com/2009/07/12/business/12corner.html?_r=1&emc=eta1.

APPRECIATIONS

One of my teachers used to tell students, "If you think you are enlightened, have dinner with your family. They'll teach you what you *still* need to learn about yourself." The same could be said about writing a book. If you think you know yourself, your work, your friends or clients—write a book. You will learn more than you ever realized about their talents and their personal stories. And you will discover what you didn't know you didn't know about yourself that you still need to learn and have the courage to share.

Much of what is in this book started out as common-sense intuition for me. I navigated through life assimilating what works while being curious about what doesn't work. Along the way I learned that it takes friends, clients, family, and newfound like-minded thinkers—and some doubting souls—to make the invisible, intuitive way of seeing things become visible. That's what so many people helped me do in bringing this book of ideas to you.

There would be no book without the unwavering faith of my friend and colleague Logan Loomis, who persistently encouraged me (for years) to bring the Power of Pause to life. Suzie Hise thoughtfully read every version of the manuscript, making sure that the practices she had seen work in organizations would help readers handle what's on their plate. Peter Shaplen is my oldest friend and a masterful storyteller who had the patience and courage to challenge me to dig deeper into what I meant to say. (Peter, now it's your turn to take the pen!)

Edgar and Santina Lorch generously opened unforgettable (*indimenticabile*) international windows to help me understand the urgent need to bring the Power of Pause practices to life in many cultures. I had no idea that my wise friend Fred Norwood is an editor extraordinaire—able to draw ideas out of me in a high-speed verbal dance. Ted Theodores contributed his love of words and ideas to making sure that these principles "syncromesh" with everyday business realities.

As a provost, chancellor, and university president, Mark Rosenberg hasn't hesitated to use these concepts in bold ways and dared me to "let the book happen." I appreciate that executives Steve Hayworth, Anne Wass, Jeff and Gary Saunders, Joe Wyson, Ellen Blattel, David Rose, Carol Cone, Kerry Rapport, Jens Bang, and many members of Young Presidents Organization Forum groups were early adopters of these practices. They demonstrated that regardless of your title or what you think you know, you never stop learning. Thanks also to Bob Tobias, who contributed the opening story with a powerful insight gained early in his career. Many other storytellers in the book shared candid lessons, including Bobby Bendetson and Joyce Elam, who demonstrate that the impossible *is* possible when you come to the fork in the road.

Kimberly Taylor and Nathan Hiller, professors at Florida International University College of Business Administration, generously provided constructive insights in the midst of busy teaching and research schedules. My brother Ken Guilmartin, founder of Music Together, and dear friend Lyn Ransom helped advance the Power of Pause curriculum by inviting me to teach in their innovative organization.

Tom Goodgame, former president of Westinghouse Broadcasting Television Station Group, is the kind of boss who

teaches you lessons for life, lessons that you find yourself passing on to others year after year. His support for the uncon-
ventional ways we sought to pioneer solutions to local and
national problems enabled dedicated colleagues, viewers,
community leaders, and sponsors to make a lasting difference.
Early in my career, advice from Francine Achbar and Mike
Wheeler helped me learn when it was time to speak up and
when it was wiser to listen. In those days, Kenneth Blanchard
and Spencer Johnson's book, *The One Minute Manager*,
was a big help when I was suddenly promoted to lead eight
people in a 24/7 workplace. Thanks to Jay Winsten's efforts
at the Harvard School of Public Health, the partnership
with Westinghouse flourished, and the Designated Driver
Program became a nationally accepted idea.

Senator Paul Tsongas and his chief of staff, Dennis
Kanin, taught me that the courage of one's convictions tem-
pered by humility is key to making a difference, especially
in trying times. John Scherer and Jan Smith are leadership
educators who challenge you to the core while inspiring you
to unlock the hidden talents of others. I am grateful to author
Pema Chodron for her compassionate, down-to-earth writing
that restores peace of mind in the midst of uncertainty. Then
there is Margaret Wheatley, whose *Leadership and the New
Science* reminds us to have faith that order will emerge if we
can learn to trust one another in the chaos. Thanks also go to
the writers and editors of the *Boston Globe* sports pages, whose
commitment to revealing the human stories of owners, managers, teammates, and rivals reminds us that long after a game is
won or lost, there is *always more to a story* than meets the eye.

Moshe Hammer, founder of From Violence to Violins,
is a longtime friend and entrepreneur whose finely tuned

ear can exquisitely distinguish whether or not a cherished idea rings true. Suzanne Rothwell, David Borer, and Janet Miller offered reality checks—about being effective in a 24/7 world while also honoring the people you work with. I'm grateful to discover my friend Hank Riefle's hidden talent for deconstructing stories to their essence. Lieutenant Colonel Edward Pfeffer, U.S. Army (retired) provided thoughtful, timely input.

Then there are the thousands of people I'd never met before who came to programs where I was teaching people about *Healing Conversations* and what to say when you don't know what to say or do in life's inevitably difficult moments. When I'd ask, "What's one thing that you learned that was of value today?" people wouldn't hesitate to answer. They'd say that putting in the clutch to pause was something they'd remember, or that the idea of getting curious not furious could keep them out of trouble. Others said that just asking themselves what they didn't know they didn't know would give them a new way to see a problem. They'd turn to ask me, "Why don't you write these ideas down so we can pass them along?"

Then there was the support of Sheryl Fullerton (my editor), Liz Kay, Nan Gardetto, Ron Bordelon, Jan Nickerson, Jeannie Lindheim, Greg Dix, Carlyn Jefford, Mary Ann Sprinkle, Christine Felix, Karen Ellenbecker, Roger Turgeon, and my other Business Network International (BNI) colleagues for my book *Healing Conversations* that enabled me to introduce these ideas to audiences and readers. Emilia Nuccio is just as passionate about bringing the Power of Pause into people's lives.

Many hands touch a book before it reaches you. My agent, Doris Michaels, and her talented assistant, Delia

Berrigan, believe in their writers and help us give birth to successful books. Editors Karen Murphy, Erin Moore, and Michele Jones know when to push and when to pull one's treasured ideas into sharper focus. The Jossey-Bass teams care about authors and do their best to transform words and images into a practical resource for you. Kudos to Mary Garrett and Gayle Mak! David Hahn, of Planned Television Arts, mobilized his public relations and marketing teams to pioneer new ways to reach time-pressed readers.

Then there are the gifted professionals who help you endure the stress of writing for thousands of hours: many thanks to healers Susan Atwood, Dr. Bob Videyko, Dr. John Johansson, Kathy O'Connor, Dr. Jonathan March, and John Wile, as well as to my "computer doctor," Andy Agapow, and my thoughtful attorney, Roberta Fitzsimmons.

Of course family members put up with what we think we know, and smile when we realize we don't know it all. What you say, how you think, what you do, and how you appreciate one another count more than you may ever know. My parents, along with Laurie and James, Kirk and Pam, David, Arielle and Adrianna, Kathleen and Paul, know what I mean. I'm also blessed with special people who allowed me to "adopt" them as extended family. Connie, Gordon and Brion, Pat and Jim, Valeria, Rosa, and Byrd and Alice—thank you from the bottom of the learning curve.

ABOUT THE AUTHOR

Nance Guilmartin is a four-time regional Emmy Award–winning journalist, business adviser, nationally known keynote speaker, and leadership educator. She works with organizations and individuals, teaching them to unlock hidden opportunities and to succeed in a time-challenged world of change. She is a Fellow of the Center for Leadership at Florida International University and was awarded an appointment as Clinical Adjunct Professor in the School of Management and International Business. Her first book, *Healing Conversations: What to Say When You Don't Know What to Say,* published in over a dozen languages, is a "communications first-aid kit" to enhance readers' abilities to respond to life's inevitably difficult moments—at work, at home, and in the community.

As a Westinghouse Broadcasting senior executive, she launched national public-private partnerships, including the Designated Driver Program and the nationally syndicated *For Kids' Sake* and Time to Care campaigns. Prior to her television career, she served as press secretary to the late Senator Paul Tsongas and was a writer-producer for CBS WEEI/Newsradio. She is a graduate of Tufts University, where she learned to value the art of asking the right questions and telling "truth to power." Please visit http://www.nanceguilmartin.com/ for information about strengths-based professional development. This includes strategic counsel or just-in-time executive coaching, interactive, "hear it today, use it tomorrow" keynotes, hands-on continuing education programs, and time-sensitive organizational consulting or customized off-sites and retreats.

INDEX

A

Action: consequences of
rushed, 32–33; when to
pause before taking,
36–37, 47
Aggression, 157, 223n1
Ahtissari, Marti, 185
Alawi, Ali, 183
Amazon, customer service
experience at, 91–92
American Association for
Cancer Research (AACR),
178–179, 224n3
Anbender, Ken, 220n1
Anchoring, 88–89
Anger: controlling, fueled by
resentments, 149–152; in
customer service work,
89–90; Get Curious Not
Furious approach to
defusing, 60–62, 107–108;
as inappropriate mindset
for responding, 59; leading
to insight vs. action, 58–59;
pausing to get beyond,
42–45; as response to time
pressures, 55

Appreciations: giving, as Power
of Pause practice, 197–198,
202, 213; tips for giving
and accepting, 208–210;
workplace transformed by,
199–201
Ariely, Dan, 56
Assumptions: checking,
as component of
communication intelligence,
41–42; questioning, when
expectations not met,
48; suspending, with Get
Curious Not Furious
approach, 59, 84
Athletes: managing, using
pause, 203–207; pausing to
examine poor performance,
101–102
Attention: continuous
partial, 6–7, 119–120, 219n1;
deficit disorder, 65; filters'
impacting, 68–69
Attitude: of curiosity, 84;
importance of, 42, 47
Attitude adjustment
accelerator, 153–154

INDEX

Knowledge: and leadership, 114–115; obsolete, 116
Konstantakatou, Anastasia, 182

L
Landon, Kirk, 179
Leadership: based on collaboration, 190; curiosity employed to solve conflict with, 96–100; dependencies understood by, 115–116; and knowledge, 114–115; tips for agility by, 100–101
Learning: education to provide framework for, 189–190; importance of, to mind, 162–163
Lehrer, Jonah, 56–57
Lencioni, Patrick, 75, 140
Listening: in collaborative cancer research, 172–173; in customer service, 94; filters' impact on, 67–69; by leaders, 137–138; while impaired, 161. *See also* Rephrasing; Reverse rephrasing
Loomis, Logan, 153
Luechtefeld, Monica, 192, 193–195

M
Maharaj, Mac, 182, 184, 185
Markova, Dawna, 80

Massarotti, Tony, 206
McGuinness, Martin, 186, 187, 188
Meunier, Joe, 199–201
Meyer, Roelf, 182, 186
Mindset: for communication intelligence, 41–42, 79; defined, 41; for rephrasing, 78; for reverse rephrasing, 154–155
Miscommunication: comedy routine about, 39–40; due to cultural differences, 173; humans wired for, 161; as "missed understandings," 66; reasons for frequency of, 62–65
Moore, Harold (Hal), 22–24

N
Naisbitt, John, 78
Nocera, Joe, 91–92
Novak, David, 209
Nowak, Martin, 170
Nurses, value of pause for, 17–20

O
Obama, Barack, 192
Office Depot, 193–195
O'Malley, Padraig, 184, 185, 186

240

P

Padilla, Ramon, 122, 124–125

Papelbon, Jonathan, 101–102, 216

Pause: for appreciations, 197–198, 202, 209–210; choice of, vs. reaction, 8, 31; consequences of acting without, 32–33; controlling resentments with, 149–152; cues for taking, 46–48; for dealing with time pressures, 1–2; described, 21; discovering power of, 13–14; improved decision making with, 22–24; innovation encouraged by, 80–82; overcoming objections to using, 48–51; paradox of, 35–37; problem solving improved by, 30, 32, 36–37; setting example of, 20; time required for, 49; and understanding how people change, 188, 188–189

Pedroia, Dustin "Pedey," 203–204

Power of Pause: author's experiences developing, 3–5; in globalized work world, 216–217; as phrase to remember, 217; practices for implementing, 212–213

Prioritizing, 122–125, 213

Problem solving: and expression of problem, 89; improved by pause, 30, 32, 36–37; and solving the right problem, 73–76; and understanding the problem, 96–100

Proust, Marcel, 79, 190

Q

Questions, importance of asking right, 25–28. *See also What don't I know I don't know* question; *What's on your plate* question

R

Race car metaphor: "drive-by" conversations in, 32; pause in, 29–30, 31; stripping the gears in, 32–33

Ramaphosa, Cyril, 187, 188

Ratey, John, 65

Reaction: choice of, vs. pause, 8, 31; danger of immediate, to e-mails, 27; gaining control over patterns of, 156–157; immediate, due to time pressures, 14–15; overcoming habit of automatic, 84–85; question to ask before, 153–154; from resentments, 148–149, 149–152

Relaxation response, 30, 32

Technology: collaboration needed for innovation based on, 193–195; collaborative government based on, 192; continuous partial attention due to, 119–120; disruptive, 113–114; miscommunication facilitated by, 62–66; time pressure with, 14–15
Teichman, Sherman, 181, 183
Tetlock, Philip, 57
Thoreau, Henry David, 83
Tilly, Charles, 90
Time: required for pause, 49; required for rephrasing, 104–105; shortage of, 14–15; and stress, 51
Time pressures: possible responses to, 55; Power of Pause for dealing with, 1–2, 6–7; reverse rephrasing when facing, 143–145
Time urgency impatience, 63–64
Tobias, Bob, 13–14
Trigger points: exercise for becoming aware of, 149, 157–158; knowing, as Power of Pause practice, 156–157, 213; resentments as, 148–149
Trust, building: with appreciations, 198, 202; with rephrasing, 77, 105, 212

Tsongas, Paul, 4
Tuncer, Murat, 176

U
Ulman, Howard, 207
Ury, William, 37

V
Venting, 59, 97, 101, 108
Veritek, Jason, 205–206

W
Westinghouse Broadcasting, 4, 85, 122
What don't I know I don't know question: in bottleneck meeting, 134; examples of impact of using, 217–218; as phrase to remember, 217; as Power of Pause practice, 128–131, 213; and resentments, 150; tips for using, 153–154
What's on your plate question, 122–125, 213
"Who's on First?" (Abbott and Costello), 39–40, 220n3
Wile E. Coyote moments, 52
Woodson, Sally, 92–94
Work Smarter Together, Not Harder program, 122–123

Y
Yan, Lijing L., 63